AT HOME
with DOGS
and their
DESIGNERS

AT HOME
with DOGS
and their
DESIGNERS

SHARING A STYLISH LIFE

SUSANNA SALK

Principal Photography by STACEY BEWKES
Foreword by ROBERT COUTURIER

RIZZOLI
NEW YORK

New York · Paris · London · Milan

CONTENTS

This book is dedicated to all the dogs out
there who have not yet found loving homes.
May its subjects inspire people to adopt them
and soon discover how enriched their
rooms and lives will become.

FOREWORD

by Robert Couturier

I can't imagine a life without dogs. A dog is beautiful to you the same way any child is beautiful to his or her parents. Of course, I look forward to seeing my husband, Jeffrey, on the weekends, but when I arrive and the dogs are bounding up to greet me, it's the greatest happiness in my life. Dogs are an extension of ourselves; they represent the best part of us.

We have four dogs, all Shih Tzus—Hercule, the oldest; Dora, six years old and a rescue dog whose early life was so horrible that we make sure she has a perfect life now; Clara, three years old; and Zazou, two years old—and four more are buried in our garden. Our dogs are a huge part of our lives. When I have breakfast, they all sit next to me, in order of age. I have chairs for each of them. We don't feed them from the table (well, when Jeffrey isn't looking, I may slip them a treat). When I go out at night, I always make sure to come home on time to care for them. I worry about them. I even leave the TV on for them when we are out.

I don't design for the dogs. A dog is a dog. They've chewed up the bases of a couple chairs, and now and then maybe there is an accident. While that doesn't make me happy, in the big picture, it doesn't really matter. You have to be careful with Shih Tzus because they hold resentments. One of ours, Bess, always pooped in the dining room when she was unhappy with something we'd done. She always knew exactly where to do it so Jeffrey would step in it! I don't

change my design to suit the dogs, though some people probably do. I make sure the dogs are comfortable. I give them silk velvet to sit on and I don't worry about their wet paws. When you're responsible for an animal's life, you have to make it the best life possible.

I find that the nicest people have the nicest dogs. I have clients who even have little dog steps for their dogs to climb onto the bed. Sometimes a client will say to me that he or she will never have a dog, and then the client gets one and falls completely in love with it. They treat it like his or her child, just as we do.

I've never chosen a dog for its decorative qualities; you get your dogs because you love them. I grew up with a miniature poodle, my mother's dog. She was a wonderful little dog and incredibly intelligent. I realized my mother had no heart when she let the dog die at the vet on her own. The four dogs we've had and lost have all died in my arms.

As you'll see in this wonderful book from Susanna Salk, I am not the only interior designer obsessed with my pooches—there are dozens of us! While fine design and dogs might seem mutually exclusive, a perusal of this book—or many of my fellow designers' Instagram feeds—quickly reveals quite the opposite. No matter how haute the couture—from Carolyne Roehm to Kelly Wearstler, Martyn Bullard to Jonathan Adler—their dogs are almost a part of the decor, and certainly a big part of their lives. From Steven Gambrel's

sidekick, Sailor, to Schuyler Samperton's beloved Tricky, dogs are what make a house a home—and humans a family. These designers are proof that anyone can have—and adore—a dog, no matter how elevated his or her environs. The dogs seem to know how fortunate they are to be in such splendid surroundings, and they rise to the occasion. And we humans certainly know how lucky we are to have our furry friends' love and devotion.

I've had the pleasure of knowing and working with Susanna Salk for many years. She has incredible vitality and positivity; it's wonderful working on projects with her. Susanna has three rescue dogs of her own, and while our Shih Tzus are pampered indoor pets, hers are the more typical, but just as beloved, outdoorsy dogs. Susanna is the perfect person to write this book, proving, like all the designers shown here, that it is possible to be devoted not only to design at the highest levels but also to the four-legged creatures who share our beautiful homes—and, if truth be told, who rule the roost.

INTRODUCTION

by Susanna Salk

It is surprising that so many interior designers and dogs are able to share a stylish life together because practically speaking, a *Régence* chair upholstered in velveteen silk, a Chinese art deco bench, creamy linen bedsheets, or any other deliciously delicate decor detail can't cohabit with a dog's muddy paw prints, shedding, and chewing. And yet, I can't think of a group who embraces the often crazy and chaotic canine world more than interior designers. Why? Because they of all people understand that beautiful rooms don't resonate— indeed, they don't even feel comfortable—if they lack soul. And what's more soulful than the sight of your dog joyously greeting you at the front door with its tail wagging furiously or soothingly curled up at the foot of your bed? Dogs can make your home feel more complete than the chicest carpet, curtain, or chintz ever could. Designers know this as surely as they choose between a solid and a stripe.

Inside these pages, you won't see precious purebred lap dogs, whose roles are to be admired until they interfere with more formal socializing and then are discreetly removed. Instead, you will meet dogs of all pedigrees and personalities, often rescued from shelters, living large (no matter how small) at home. They snooze, feast, romp, cuddle (and yes, sometimes pee and poo) in some of the chicest rooms in the world. The privilege they enjoy is really more about the unconditional love bestowed upon them, rather than the materialistic riches offered.

When I sent out my ask letter inviting these twenty-two designers—some of the world's very best—to participate in this book, I heard back from all of them within the hour (some just minutes) with a resounding "YES!" If I had given them the choice of featuring their latest project on the cover of a book called *Chicest Rooms Ever*, I believe the response would have taken longer. I think that because as exciting as it is to have work published, deep down we all want to share and celebrate our profound love for family even more.

And as lucky as the designers and the dogs are who are profiled, it is important to remember that there are still so many deserving dogs who haven't found a home yet. I hope this book inspires you to make a home for one of the thousands of dogs already out there who are waiting to give love—and rescue all of us in return.

FOXY AND FABULOUS IN GREENWICH VILLAGE

by Jonathan Adler

Foxy: sassy tail

Angelic face, russet hue

We super love you.

FoxyLady

AGE: A lady never tells (especially a lady rescued from a shelter who isn't quite sure) BREED: Mutt

FOXYLADY'S HOMES: Foxy splits her time between New York City and Shelter Island, with the occasional jaunt to Palm Beach.

Potter, designer, and author Jonathan Adler and author,
window dresser, and fashion commentator Simon Doonan
share their homes with FoxyLady. Above: FoxyLady loves to
perch on the vintage gold Pedro Friedeberg chairs beneath
the Cindy Sherman photograph.

RIGHT
Jonathan gives FoxyLady a break by carrying her through the
dining room, replete with his designed Lucite dog bed.

TIPS ON LIVING A STYLISH LIFE

On Character

Stuff is just stuff. The truth is everything we own is partially gnawed on (whether by FoxyLady or Simon, who knows). It adds character.

On Adoption by Any Other Name

Don't not adopt a dog from a shelter just because you don't like its given name. FoxyLady's name used to be Martha.

On Stylish Snaps

Don't be afraid to get up close and personal, not to mention on all fours. The best pictures are the ones that feel as if they were taken from a dog's-eye view. FoxyLady always seems to find the best light in any room.

On Collars and Outfits

Never a collar for FoxyLady. She is usually in the nude. Think odalisque. For rainy weather, her camouflage raincoat gives her an edgy look that says, "Don't f*ck with me, fellas." When you're this beautiful, you have to be tough.

▶ On Ladies Who Lunch

A lady never said no to a nibble of roast chicken, especially when it is served in my Lucite and brass dog bowl.

On Haute Couture Snoozing

FoxyLady loves snoozing curled up in her bed in Simon's office, with one of his old Burberry scarves as he works on his latest page-turner.

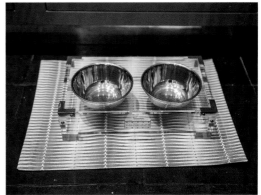

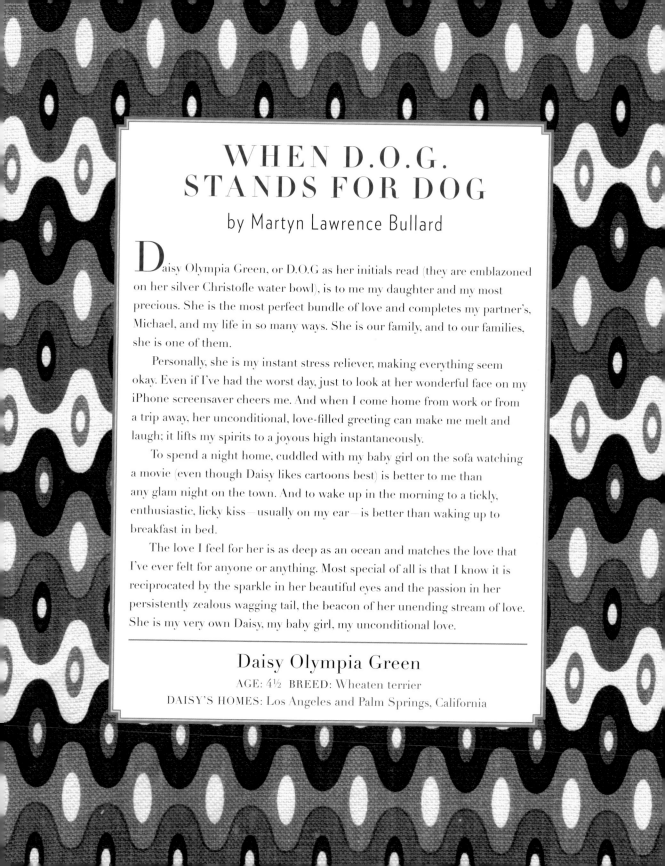

WHEN D.O.G. STANDS FOR DOG

by Martyn Lawrence Bullard

Daisy Olympia Green, or D.O.G as her initials read (they are emblazoned on her silver Christofle water bowl), is to me my daughter and my most precious. She is the most perfect bundle of love and completes my partner's, Michael, and my life in so many ways. She is our family, and to our families, she is one of them.

Personally, she is my instant stress reliever, making everything seem okay. Even if I've had the worst day, just to look at her wonderful face on my iPhone screensaver cheers me. And when I come home from work or from a trip away, her unconditional, love-filled greeting can make me melt and laugh; it lifts my spirits to a joyous high instantaneously.

To spend a night home, cuddled with my baby girl on the sofa watching a movie (even though Daisy likes cartoons best) is better to me than any glam night on the town. And to wake up in the morning to a tickly, enthusiastic, licky kiss – usually on my ear – is better than waking up to breakfast in bed.

The love I feel for her is as deep as an ocean and matches the love that I've ever felt for anyone or anything. Most special of all is that I know it is reciprocated by the sparkle in her beautiful eyes and the passion in her persistently zealous wagging tail, the beacon of her unending stream of love. She is my very own Daisy, my baby girl, my unconditional love.

Daisy Olympia Green

AGE: 4½   BREED: Wheaten terrier
DAISY'S HOMES: Los Angeles and Palm Springs, California

Interior designer and author Martyn Lawrence Bullard and
property developer and vintage dealer Michael Green share their
Los Angeles and Palm Springs homes with Daisy. Above: Daisy
and Martyn enjoy teatime in the Moroccan-inspired dining niche.

RIGHT
Daisy loves this Mansour Berber rug in the living room and often
blissfully uses it as her own scratching pad.

OPPOSITE

Daisy considers the guest room her space. Occasionally she is known to share
the bed with a guest or two.

ABOVE

Daisy's favorite spot in the garden is perched upon the Moroccan leather poofs
where she can see all the comings and goings of the house. Later she will curl up
on the deep outdoor benches, nuzzling into the Schumacher outdoor fabric.

TIPS ON LIVING A STYLISH LIFE

On Designing with Dogs in Mind

My interiors are designed for living: they may seem glamorous, but at their heart is always comfort. This rule applies to all who live within them, and dogs are no exception. I always try to take into account their needs and comfort in the design process.

▲ On Collars and Bling

Collars are practical but also function as great pieces of jewelry. Daisy's snakeskin collar decorated with rhinestones and an enameled daisy charm from Tiffany suit her name and personality.

◄ On Bringing the Outdoors In

To allow a carefree environment for my dog-loving clients, I will often use outdoor fabrics and rugs on indoor furnishings and floors. Today's amazing manufacturing techniques offer up a startling array of chic choices that fool the eye and touch, thus allowing my luxe look to prevail while giving homeowners assurance that even if their beloved dog has a mishap, all will be fine due to stain-free and easy-to-clean materials.

▶ On Dog-Friendly Fabrics

Remember that with today's technology, fabrics and furnishings can be treated with nontoxic protective sprays and coatings that repel watermarks and stains and provide easy cleaning of even the most delicate of fabrics. There's a wide variety of companies that come to your home to do this, and we often offer the service before installing our upholstery.

On Leather and Fur

Leather is always an easy choice for our furry friends to make their own spot upon. I will always try to incorporate a leather club chair or two into the family and living rooms so the dog has a seat of its very own to enjoy the evening with the family. In fact, Daisy has her own black leather club chair (now her namesake in my furniture line), complete with brass studs that complement her complexion.

◀ On Playing Hide-and-Seek

Daisy's toys live piled under an eighteenth-century Italian cabinet. She loves to dig in and find her favorite toy of the week, which she will play with and then hide back in the pile.

HAPPY IN HANCOCK PARK

by Betsy Burnham

My dogs are totally spoiled. They get walked twice a day; they sun in the backyard on snappy little outdoor cushions; they sleep in our room; they've been to Mexico. The eldest, crankiest one gets acupuncture for her aches and pains and is driven in the car so she can hang out the window and feel like a puppy again. The smallest, most fearful one gets held in someone's arms—often for hours—when we have parties. The youngest—an adorable rescue—stares deeply into our eyes, anxious every minute that this new country-club life he stumbled into may somehow vanish when one of us leaves the room.

Dogs—even my occasionally poorly behaved pack—possess all the traits that each of us works so hard to get right in our lifetime: authenticity, loyalty, patience, optimism; unbridled happiness in response to even the smallest things; acceptance of others; generosity of emotion; and unfailing, unconditional love. I find it inspiring.

And the thing is: All the extravagant stuff? That's really just for me because it doesn't matter to them. All my dogs really want is for us to be and to stay—to offer them a lap, some praise, or a belly rub. My dog Nina Garcia sits behind me on my chair every day I'm in my office. She'll miss a meal just to be with me.

I'll keep spoiling Lola, Nina Garcia, and Felix because it makes me feel good. And I can't imagine our house without them. Forget the furniture, wallpaper, and pretty stuff—it's the dogs that make it a home.

Lola	Nina Garcia	Felix
AGE: 12 BREED: Smooth-coat Chihuahua	AGE: 11 BREED: Long-haired Chihuahua	AGE: 3 BREED: Mix of Shih Tzu, Pomeranian, and poodle

LOLA, NINA GARCIA, AND FELIX'S HOME: A 1927 Roland Coate–designed house in the Hancock Park area of Los Angeles.

ℰℓℓℯ

Interior designer Betsy Burnham, her husband, television producer Mark Stern, and their
children, Carson and Will Stern, when they are home from school, share their home with Lola,
Nina, and Felix. It's got a great backyard with sunny spots to hang out in. Opposite: Nina and
Felix are the first to greet visitors at the front door. The square space is open to hallways and
rooms on all sides, so the vintage zebra hide is the perfect entry rug.

ABOVE

A back corner of the living room, where all the furniture pieces are vintage. Nina looks
particularly fetching beneath the Rose Cumming fabric-covered lamp shade.

TIPS ON LIVING A STYLISH LIFE

On Leaning In

It's entirely possible to live both with dogs and beautiful things but I think two things have to happen: First, train your dogs. This does not happen overnight, nor is it easy—but if you work at it, it's definitely in the realm of possibility. Second, relax. Living with dogs also means everything can't be one hundred-percent perfect all the time, so lean into this and just enjoy it. I encourage everyone to really live in their homes—with kids, with dogs, and with company.

On Understanding Accidents

Relax a little. Accidents happen. Pet hair happens. In my opinion, snuggling on the sofa with my dogs is worth it.

▶ On Collars and Leashes

For walks, Lola wears a green-striped collar and leash from Harry Barker. She used to wear Louis Vuitton but grew out of it. Mark feels this extravagance was insane anyway, so we did not purchase a second one. Nina's collar is black-and-white gingham. She also wears a harness for walks because she never finished obedience classes. Lola can be a bit of a "little monster" because she never stays on the sidewalk. Felix is partial to his blue gingham, which he gets filthy in no time.

▲ On Camo and Vintage

Felix loves his camo dog bed by Fatboy, while Nina
and Lola take turns on a vintage chair in the entry
hall covered in Kravet's Gaban Stripe Sundance
from their Museum of New Mexico collection. The
vintage runner is from Aga John.

▶ On Keeping Fun Accessible

Toys are kept neat and organized in shallow
baskets throughout the house so they're accessible
by dogs and humans alike.

▶ On Being Individual

Being individuals, dogs have preferences for where
they sleep. Lola prefers a little bed that is way
too small for her. It is kept in the laundry room.
If she's in a good mood, she'll snuggle under
the covers of our bed, which is simultaneously a
treat and an annoyance because she is a snorer.
Nina can only sleep if her body is in contact with
a human. Felix is not picky and will relax on any
type of dog bed situated just about anywhere.

▲ On Homemade Food

Our housekeeper, Ana, and I make meals for our
dogs. They are partial to poached chicken (breast
meat only) served with kibble.

AVOIR DU CHIEN IN CONNECTICUT

by Robert Couturier

There is not a time in my life where I have been without a dog or not loving a dog—or many dogs. I have a passion for small dogs especially; the love in their eyes and the complete trust in you when you lift them up and hug them is the purest form of joy I have ever felt.

My mother's dog—a miniature poodle, who loved me exclusively and whom I would put in a backpack wrapped up in scarves when I went skiing—followed me everywhere. She died at fifteen and I still have her wonderful scent in my nose.

When my adult life became more settled, I decided to get a Shih Tzu, and I did what a responsible dog owner should never do: I walked into the pet shop on Lexington Avenue and I left with two Shih Tzus, one black and one gray. They became Chuck and Lili, and I loved them more than I thought I was capable of loving.

Later Jeffrey—my partner, whom I was going to marry when that became allowed—and I got Henriette (while Chuck and Lili were 7). Lili was so upset that I had to take her on drives alone with me so she could still think that she was the only one who owned my heart (in truth she was and still is). When Chuck and Lili died, I buried them in my gardens, both in mahogany boxes wrapped in their cashmere blankets and surrounded by their favorite toys.

Whenever one of our dogs die, we replace him or her with another: we have Hercule who took Chuck's place, then Bess, who took Lili's, and Clara, who took Bess's. This never meant that I would forget the one who had died, of course.

Hercule
AGE: 9 BREED: Shih Tzu

Clara
AGE: 3 BREED: Shih Tzu

Dora
AGE: 6 BREED: Shih Tzu

Zazou
AGE: 2 BREED: Shih Tzu

THE DOGS' HOME: Kent, Connecticut

Four years before Henriette passed away, Dora came into our life. And, Zazou joined us over two years ago.

One day a friend of mine who works at the ASPCA sent me a note saying, "I know you love your Shih Tzus but this is what some people do." This is how I met Dora—she had been rescued from a horribly, cruelly, inhumanly abusive life and was a few days from dying. Of course, I called Jeffrey crying telling him that we were going to have a fourth dog and I went to meet her. She was shaking like a leaf but when I took her in my arms, she was home and she knew nothing bad would ever happen to her again.

Dogs are the better parts of our souls as they never lie, they never betray, they never falter, and they never disappoint. They love us unconditionally whether or not we are in a good mood or we have bad breath. I will never live without dogs as they truly make my world beautiful and the unavoidable unhappiness bearable. My dogs who have died—Tina, Lili, Chuck, Bess, and Henriette—still are fully present in my heart, where they'll live as long as I do. I don't believe in heaven or hell, but if there are such things then heaven is full of dogs and hell is without them.

Interior designer, architect, and author Robert Couturier and pre-Revolutionary America decorative art expert and architectural preservationist Jeffrey Morgan share their home with Hercule, Clara, Dora, and Zazou. Above: Here, the dogs enjoy the manicured gardens behind the main house.

RIGHT
In the master bedroom, an English nineteenth-century dog-head piggy bank graces a side table.

OPPOSITE
The dogs get cozy on a fur throw atop a Fortuny fabric–covered French Louis XVI daybed by Jacob. The eighteenth-century portrait is by American painter Ralph Earl.

TIPS ON LIVING
A STYLISH LIFE

▸ On Where Dogs Are Welcome

I live with my dogs as I would without them. Dogs are
welcome anywhere and on anything (maybe not on dining
room tables) but certainly on all sofas, beds, daybeds,
and armchairs.

On *Petits* Accidents

Accidents happen with or without dogs. People can spill
red wine and dogs can vomit. Life is messy. Things go
wrong with us, and things go wrong with dogs—there is no
difference. (By the way my dogs have never broken anything,
unlike my staff and guests.)

On Being Covered

In our newly fashioned mudroom, we
have covered the floor with wall-to-wall
matting, which is ideal for little wet paws
and big wet feet. There are towels to dry
the dogs.

On Living with
Beautiful Things

I love all my things and I live surrounded
by what I love, dogs—with all their
shortcomings—included. I will not park
them somewhere or forbid them to go
where I go. When accidents happen, we
wipe them up, clean them up, forget about
them, and go on living with our beloved dogs.

▸ On Clothes and Collars

Our dogs love being nude. We occasionally dress them
in brightly colored cashmere turtleneck sweaters. They
don't wear collars.

THIS SAILOR IS
ALWAYS AT HOME
by Steven Gambrel

Sailor came into our lives in the spring of 2013 when she was just four weeks old. We were at Tutto il Giorno in Sag Harbor having dinner with a group of friends when one of them asked, "What are you guys doing about a dog?" Just six months earlier, we had lost Dash, a ten-year-old Labradoodle, to hemangiosarcoma, a fast-moving form of cancer.

Our friend, whose giant Labradoodle Hobie is from Labradoodles of Long Island in Setauket, said that her breeder had a litter of puppies and that we should call to see if any were still available. The next morning we called the breeder, Eileen Hattersley, and she said yes, she had one puppy left, a sweet female, and we were welcome to stop by to meet her. And that we did. We arrived at the breeder's home and met the litter of eight puppies, who were still nursing from their mother, Madison. Then we met Madison's mother, Amber, a twelve-year-old yellow Labrador. As we were meeting the available female puppy, we made eye contact with Sailor: the most beautiful puppy we had ever seen. Although Eileen had selected her to perpetuate her line of 'doodles, after much cajoling, we convinced Eileen that we were meant to bring Sailor into our family.

We negotiated to adopt Sailor (whose name we had selected before we even met her) and then we left her with her siblings and mother for another month until she was fully weaned, vaccinated, microchipped, and ready to begin her life with us in New York City and Sag Harbor. Our time together began when we drove from the city to Setauket, picked up Sailor, and continued on our journey to Sag Harbor. That weekend included a lunch party, a boating excursion, and lots of visits from friends and family to meet Sailor. We were worried that we might overwhelm her, but she rose to each occasion and embraced the people, dogs, and experiences that were totally new to her. And the past three years have been a nonstop life of workdays in my office in Soho, weekend trips to Sag Harbor, semiannual vacations with her grandparents in Virginia, and more love and adoration than she could possibly absorb.

Sailor Anderson Gambrel

AGE: 5 BREED: Labradoodle SAILOR'S HOMES: New York City
and Sag Harbor, New York

Interior designer, architect, and author Steven Gambrel and James Anderson, principal of grayANDERSON, a real-estate branding and marketing company, share their townhouse in New York City's West Village and a historic sea captain's house in Sag Harbor, New York, with Sailor. Opposite: With a view of the front door of the townhouse, Sailor favors the library as a midmorning hangout.

ABOVE
Style over comfort—this sofa with a tight back and seat is rarely chosen as a perch. The large abstract painting of birds is by Maria Kozak.

ABOVE

This early nineteenth-century English dog collar was
purchased in London at an antiques fair as a gift for Sailor;
she finds it a bit pretentious and unwieldy.

OPPOSITE

The staircase is original to the townhouse. Crooked and
full of character, it is covered in red sisal, which is good for
traction and not too precious for muddy paws.

ooooo

TIPS ON LIVING A STYLISH LIFE

On the Importance of a Cheese Board

A cheese board finely styled on a low table, prepared for evening guests, is a family tradition, and puppies need to learn that this tempting moment is seriously off-limits, even when the dads are getting dressed upstairs. Once we have come to an agreement on this subject, puppies become family.

▲ On Choosing Silver Over Porcelain

Nineteenth-century English sterling-silver dog bowls are preferred over porcelain, which frequently breaks on stone floors. However, Sailor's multiple dog tags clink the edges something fierce when she drinks water.

▲ On Collars

Sailor loves her collar from Journeyman Saddlery in Middleburg, Virginia. It has her name and phone number engraved on a pretty brass plate.

▶ On Water Safety

Labradoodles love the water and will enter it without prompting. We discovered this the first day we took Sailor out on the boat in Sag Harbor: she jumped right in. Until we were able to train her, we made sure she was attached to a leash as soon as we got on board. We also make Sailor wear her orange life jacket when boating on *Dashaway II*, the mahogany vessel named after her predecessor, Dash.

On the Importance of Handy Towels

Sailor's love for water unfortunately does not translate to the indoors. We try and have some extra-large towels at the ready for when baths are necessary.

VELVET AND LINEN AND SHIH TZUS IN OJAI

by Brooke Giannetti

They live in the city of Ojai

With four donkeys, three goats, and a hare.

They think it's a farm called Patina

But they're not sure, to be totally fair.

Their cuteness will truly amaze you,

And they're thrilled to see Mommy come home.

But they're naughty when she isn't looking,

For any chance to get free and just roam.

They'll chew shoelaces, socks, and each other,

And they cry when they're left all alone.

But Mommy whispers and says that she loves them

Even more than the children she's sown . . .

Bebe
AGE: 12 BREED: Maltipoo

Frasier
AGE: 13 BREED: Coton de Tulear

Sera
AGE: 2 BREED: Shih Tzu

Sophie
AGE: 3 BREED: Shih Tzu

BEBE, FRASIER, SERA, AND SOPHIE'S HOME:
Patina Farm in Ojai, California

Interior designer and author Brooke Giannetti, architect Steve Giannetti, and their children Leila, Nick, and Charlie, whenever they are on college break, share their home with Bebe, Frasier, Sera, and Sophie.
Left: Sophie and Sera play near an antique Swedish tall clock.

BELOW
Sophie is obsessed with her toys. Whenever she leaves a room, she always brings a toy with her. Her duck is her favorite and oldest toy.

OPPOSITE
When the Giannettis first welcomed Sera (on the left) into their family, Sophie ignored her. Now they are inseparable.

TIPS ON LIVING A STYLISH LIFE

◀ On Fabrics that Wash and Wear Well

We use washable, natural linen slipcovers on sofas and chairs. Our vintage leather pieces are easy to clean. Vintage rugs with a tight weave work well with dogs since they don't unravel. Select rugs that are one hundred-percent wool, as stain removal is simple.

On Getting Serious about Stain Removal

We use Get Serious! extractor to remove stains before washing.

▶ On Stylish Storage

We designed a little cubby in our kitchen for dog food and bowl storage. It also provides a place for water bowls.

GOODE & BEST BRAND

DOG FOOD

Gentle food for good dogs

▲ On Being Goat Friendly

I designed my office so I could be surrounded by my animals.
The goats hang out on my porch on the other side of the steel
windows. French limestone floors are dog friendly and extend
to the goat porch beyond.

On Places to Hang Out and Sleep

The dogs appreciate their cream-colored Sherpa WallyBeds—they lounge in them all day long. At night, Sera likes to sleep curled up between Steve and me on her bed, while Sophie prefers snoozing in her Louis Vuitton carrier.

◄ On Comings and Goings

Instead of an ordinary dog gate, we use a pair of attractive antique wood cabinet doors.

OUR DOG DAISY
by Brian J. McCarthy

Truth be told, I wasn't convinced you were a good idea at first.
The thought of early morning walks when I could barely open my eyes
or late-night walks in the dead of winter or dirty paws on the carpets
or uneaten kibble tucked away in the upholstery . . . No way!
And then one early summer afternoon nine years ago they brought
    you to us and you bounced out of your crate as if you knew you
    had come home.
It was truly love at first sight for all of us.
And since that moment, I have never once minded the early morning
    walks when I could barely open my eyes or the late-night walks in
    the dead of winter or the dirty paws on the carpets
or the occasional uneaten kibble tucked away in the upholstery . . .
Because my world simply wouldn't be complete if you didn't inhabit
    it with me.

Daisy McCarthy-Sager

AGE: Surely you know better than to ask a lady her age.
BREED: Poodle mix DAISY'S HOMES: Manhattan during the week
and New York's Ulster County on weekends.

Interior designer and author Brian J. McCarthy and his partner, Danny Sager, share their homes with Daisy. Left: Daisy enjoys time alone in the living room.

ABOVE

Daisy was relieved when she realized that the woolly mammoth that arrived from Rome was not a new household pet to compete with but rather a Persian lamb Lina armchair by Fernando and Humberto Campana. She immediately made herself comfortable.

TIPS ON LIVING A STYLISH LIFE

On Being an Obsessive-Compulsive Virgo Decorator

True to my sign, I can't tolerate a mess or disorder of any sort. That being said, the greatest surprise for me since adopting Daisy nine years ago is how easily I am able to look the other way when it comes to her.

◀ On the Importance of Designated Areas

We store Daisy's treats, food, and pills in bins in a designated area to keep things simple. Her dog bed is neatly laid out by the front door with all her favorite toys.

On the Importance of Free Reign

Daisy has free reign of both our apartment and weekend home, and if she were ever inclined to make a mess (which thankfully she is not), I wouldn't even blink an eye. There is no spot in either of our homes where she is not allowed to perch or sleep or eat.

On Being *Au Naturel*

Daisy is a nudist. No silly outfits for her. A collar? Never for Daisy. She does not like the idea of being dragged around by the neck. Instead, a simple black harness works well for her.

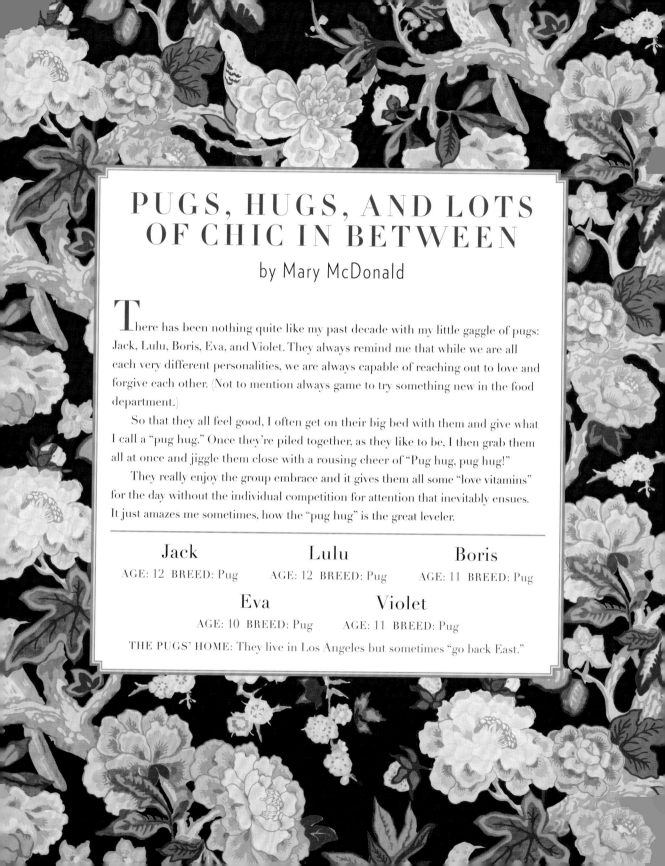

PUGS, HUGS, AND LOTS OF CHIC IN BETWEEN

by Mary McDonald

There has been nothing quite like my past decade with my little gaggle of pugs: Jack, Lulu, Boris, Eva, and Violet. They always remind me that while we are all each very different personalities, we are always capable of reaching out to love and forgive each other. (Not to mention always game to try something new in the food department.)

So that they all feel good, I often get on their big bed with them and give what I call a "pug hug." Once they're piled together, as they like to be, I then grab them all at once and jiggle them close with a rousing cheer of "Pug hug, pug hug!"

They really enjoy the group embrace and it gives them all some "love vitamins" for the day without the individual competition for attention that inevitably ensues. It just amazes me sometimes, how the "pug hug" is the great leveler.

Jack
AGE: 12   BREED: Pug

Lulu
AGE: 12   BREED: Pug

Boris
AGE: 11   BREED: Pug

Eva
AGE: 10   BREED: Pug

Violet
AGE: 11   BREED: Pug

THE PUGS' HOME: They live in Los Angeles but sometimes "go back East."

Interior designer and author Mary McDonald shares her
Los Angeles home with Jack, Lulu, Boris, Eva, and Violet.
Above: Mary's pugs enjoying a little one-on-one time
together among the blue-and-white garden jardinieres.

RIGHT
The pack awaits teatime in the drawing room.

TIPS ON LIVING
A STYLISH LIFE

On Keeping a Pack Intact

It's hard to keep track of more than two dogs, so if you have
more than that, get in the habit of doing a head count to make
sure that they are all inside. (I could accidentally take in a
raccoon and not notice, since I am satisfied once I hit five and
close the door.)

▶ On Eating Their Peas and Carrots

Dogs are omnivores, not carnivores. The trainer told me to test
raw veggies as treats when they were puppies. Mine still love
baby carrots and sweet peas—they think that carrots are dessert.
I also serve them turkey or lamb. In addition, the pugs have some
off-the-wall likes, such as Snickers bars and escargot.

◀ On the Right Leash for the Right Dog

If you have a lot of dogs, especially little ones, make sure you have enough leashes at the ready (hanging them on hooks keeps them from getting tangled). Leashes also need to be the right weight and length for your dog. A leash for a German shepherd is very different than for a pug, for example. As for collars, the girls wear red leather, and the boys dig black leather.

▶ On Where to Snuggle

My dogs love to all snuggle in a pile in the kitchen. Their special treat is to be picked as the one "snuggle dog" for the night with me. On special occasions, they all get to sleep with me.

THE MEANING OF HOME AND COAL

by Jeffrey Alan Marks

When you were first brought home, you went right for the fireplace and wouldn't come out. Your pristine white coat quickly became covered in coal. This is when you instantly personified the very name Coal.

Yes, rubbing up against my newly upholstered cashmere sofa may have started us off on the wrong foot. Yet, I admit I never realized the healing power you would eventually bring through a great deal of transition for both of us.

Chessie, with whom I had spent most of my adult life, reluctantly took you on as a sister and when she passed, you defiantly took on her gentle demeanor. Soon after, we found ourselves alone and even closer than ever. You would travel from job site to job site, always by my side; you stayed with me at the office; and when I had to travel a great deal, you protected our home.

We've hiked mountains and walked countless beaches, sharing moments that inspired my fabric and furniture collections. You've traveled on private planes and in the back of pickup trucks, and you've been lucky to experience more than most humans do. But at the close of a weekend, when we end up in the sunroom together, curled up on the daybed overlooking the ocean, this is how I believe the happiest of moments is spent.

Coal

AGE: 7 BREED: Yellow Labrador retriever
COAL'S HOME: Santa Monica Canyon, California

Interior designer, architect, and author Jeffrey Alan Marks shares his home with Coal. Opposite: Coal and Jeffrey repose in the master bedroom beneath a vintage Abercrombie & Fitch rowboat hanging from the bedroom ceiling. The bed is Jeffrey's own design, and all the fabrics and the rug are from his Kravet collection.

ABOVE

Coal rests near the old industrial English desk in front of the window with a view of the bamboo garden. The chair, an old French flea-market find, has been reconditioned and upholstered in green velvet with a lavender trim by Jeffrey.

TIPS ON LIVING A STYLISH LIFE

▲ On How Necessity is the Mother of Invention

I've always used a lot of durable indoor/outdoor fabrics throughout my house, which has inspired me to create a collection with Kravet that is completely dog friendly.

On Collars and Leashes

I prefer a houndstooth-check collar for Coal. However, for her comfort, I keep Coal's collar off when she hikes with me.

◄ On Traveling in Style

Coal travels with me a great deal so her things are held in a navy leather tote bag that matches not only the car but also the navy leash I designed for her.

On Keeping the Inside Out

Since Coal goes to the beach so often, our house has an outdoor shower we both love to use.

▶ On Running and Runners

I designed a runner for safety as Coal likes to get between my legs while going down the stairs.

▼ On Custom Cookies and Decor

I like to make Coal homemade chicken soup and doggie cookies while she hangs out on the kitchen's oak floor stained to be a match to mask shedding. The walls are covered in de Gournay's "Fishes," featuring hand-painted fish that I custom-designed.

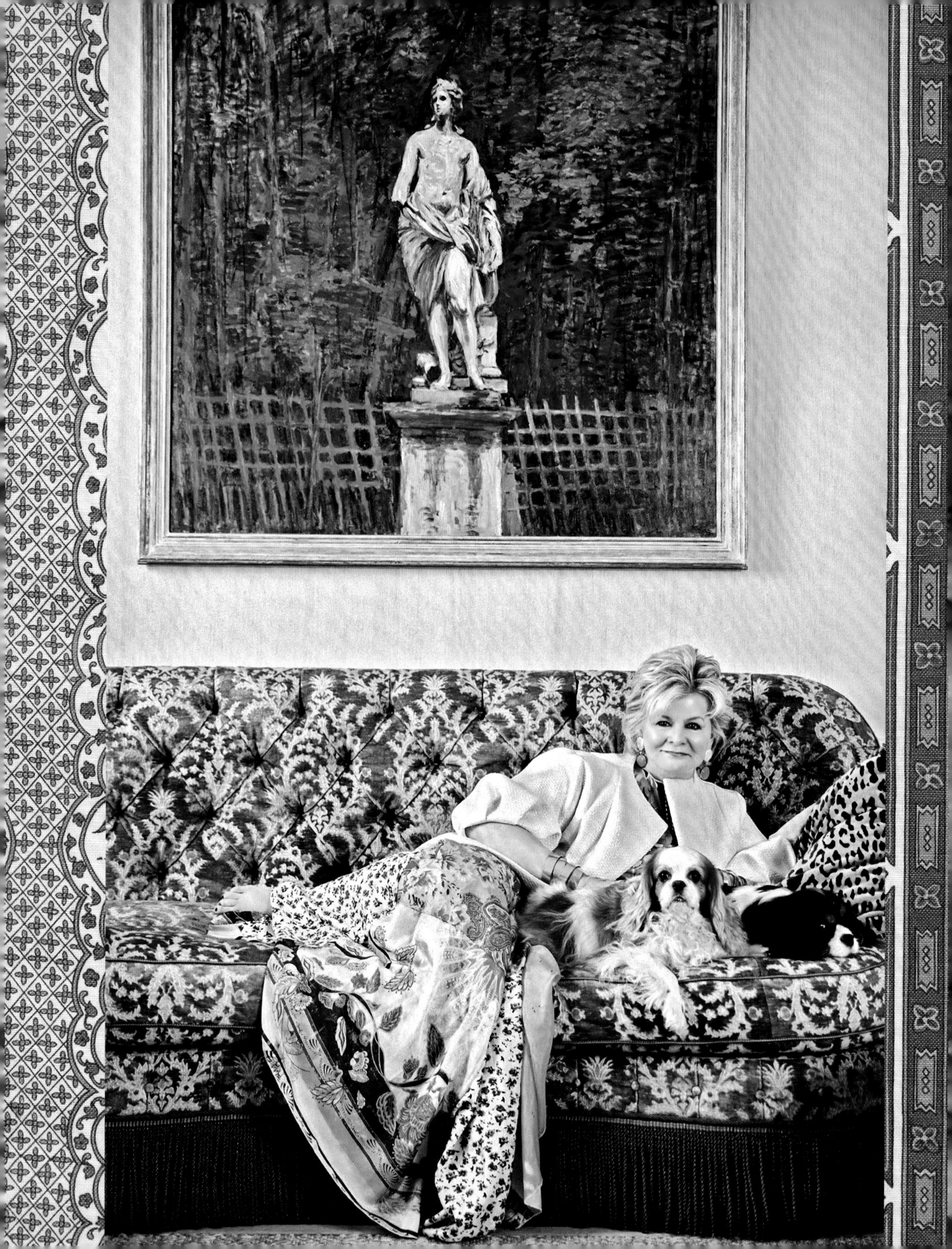

AT HOME AND AT PLAY ON THE UPPER EAST SIDE

by Charlotte Moss

Dear Daisy and Buddy,

I know as you go through life you will begin to meet friends along the way with all different types of barks. You will pass them at the park, at the groomer, on the beach, and following me around antiques shows in the country. You will meet some in school who will sit across the aisle in class and want to copy your homework and challenge you to Olympic-style events in the schoolyard. Some will invite you for sleepovers when you are a teenager, where you wake up in the morning with a tummy ache from having too many treats. There will be those you meet at camp who will be your friends for life, even if you always come in second. Then there are the special flirtations over a bowl of spaghetti.

With some friends you will simply sit under a tree and read books in perfect silence. Some of the most treasured moments may come when you decide to pack a trunk and your favorite leashes and go off on an adventure together. And while I know, like Colette said, "our perfect companions never have fewer than four feet," I hope you will always come home to this two-legged one.

Love,
Mummy

Daisy

AGE: 10 BREED: Cavalier King Charles Spaniel

Buddy

AGE: 4 BREED: Cavalier King Charles Spaniel

DAISY AND BUDDY'S HOMES: New York City and East Hampton

ℓℓℓℓ

Interior designer and author Charlotte "Char" Moss and her banker husband,
Barry Friedberg, share their homes with Daisy and Buddy. Most of the time the dogs
live in a New York City townhouse. On weekends, they often go to their country
house in East Hampton, where they have the run of the place and a yard.

OPPOSITE
The dogs always leave room for Charlotte to join them, especially in her study.

ABOVE
Charlotte and Buddy enjoy a leisurely coffee together in bed.

ℓℓℓℓℓ

ꝏℓℓℓℓ

ABOVE

Daisy and Buddy's personal preference is for the eclectic and the exotic; they commandeer a sofa as if it were their own.

LEFT

Daisy and Charlotte both head for shelter when outside in the Hamptons. Charlotte's cabana from Century Furniture is always ready for reading, talking, and napping.

OPPOSITE

Charlotte's dogs are welcome everywhere, especially in rooms where she spends a lot of time reading.

TIPS ON LIVING A STYLISH LIFE

On Staying Connected

Each dog has a leash with his or her own name. I change their leashes seasonally, just like my own wardrobe.

On Collars

Truth be told, I think of a collar like a necklace. Therefore, we have quite a collection. My friend Jane Scott Hodges (she loves accessories too) has given my dogs Fortuny collars. And then they have more casual day wear. It depends on our mood, what the day ahead looks like, and who is coming over.

▼ On Being Cozy Everywhere

Since Daisy and Buddy follow me everywhere, I try to keep a soft blanket in every room for them to lounge on.

On Classic Clothes

My dogs are pretty classic dressers, but more often than not, I just like to keep their coats clean, brushed, and silky—not covered up. When it's cold, I slip cable-knit cashmere turtlenecks on them: Daisy's is red and Buddy's is black. When it rains, they wear their patent-leather coats.

▲ On Excursions

I have a travel tote for Daisy's and Buddy's sweaters and coats and an extra leash or two. I also pack a special canvas water dish (which I found in England), a brush, a comb, and a few balls and things for the fun part.

On Staying Fabulous

I serve my dogs dry food, mixing in salmon once a week. It's great for their coats, keeping them silky and soft. Barry is more generous and sneaks them leftovers when I'm not looking. Their dinner bowls are blue-and-white porcelain, which are placed on a mat made from an antique carpet.

MORE IS MORE
IN DALLAS

by Michelle Nussbaumer

When I was a child my mother always said, "Michelle never met a dog she didn't like." That still holds true to this day. Henceforth is an ode to these four-legged friends who have joined me on this journey we call life.

To sweet Saint-John: You snuggled with me under the covers and kept me safe from all the imaginary monsters lurking under my childhood bed.

To Kubla, leader of the mongrel hordes: You were my friend and protector from the time I was seventeen years old until I was thirty-three. You stood by me through thick and thin and saved me from the burglar who broke into my college apartment. You were even there to meet my first three children, and you unconditionally loved them as well.

To Napoleone: I rescued you on the Appia Antica in Rome, along with your twelve brothers and sisters (whom I luckily found homes for), but I couldn't seem to part with you and your gentle spirit. Even though you weighed two hundred pounds, you accompanied us to Los Angeles and then Texas.

To Satchmo: You watched over all of our children as they grew, always showing infinite patience and dignity, no matter how many costumes and tutus you were forced to wear.

To my sweet Lola, my special girl: Every once in a while a unique soul enters one's life and that was you. I don't think I will ever again see such a devoted spirit and such a loving nature. I miss your noble eyes every day.

To Delilah, Gumbo, Loretta, and Winnie: You are four pranksters, and your daily antics bring joy to our lives, even though one of you killed one of my roosters. I forgive you.

To Pasha: You spoiled world-traveling regal diva, I don't think there is a country I haven't smuggled you into in my carry-on. You've been the perfect companion and I hope you still will be for many years to come.

Loretta	Tullulah	Apollonia	Pasha
BREED: Great Dane	BREED: Great Dane	BREED: Great Dane	BREED: Toy poodle

Winnie	Lobo	Rupert
BREED: Shar-Pei	BREED: German shepherd	BREED: French bulldog

AGES: Our dogs find that question offensive as age is only a number and they hate numbers. THE DOGS' HOMES: They live in Dallas, San Miguel, and Gstaad.

Interior designer and author Michelle Nussbaumer, her husband, Swiss developer Bernard Nussbaumer, and sometimes their children, Nile, Axel, Anais, and Andreas, share their homes with Loretta, Tullulah, Apollonia, Pasha, Winnie, Lobo, and Rupert. The Nussbaumers love to travel. Many of the dogs are jealous of Pasha because she gets to travel with them most often. Being a toy poodle, she can easily fit on the plane. Left: Here, she enjoys the many patterned fabrics in the living room.

BELOW
Loretta on her favorite zebra rug in Michelle's daughter's bedroom.

OPPOSITE
Rupert the Frenchie sits pretty on Michelle's chevron ikat-covered ottoman, beneath her collection of eighteenth- and nineteenth-century blue-and-white ginger jars.

To Apollonia: The rescue I found on the side of the road in Mexico, you turned into such a majestic gentle giant.

And last but not least, to my darling Great Dane Tullulah, who accompanies me to work every day and is welcomed in all the showrooms in the Design Center—from Brunschwig & Fils to Zimmer + Rohde and all those in between, usually with treats in hand. Tullulah, you are one of my dearest friends and companions in this sweet life.

I cannot imagine life without the friendship of these God's creatures. They are always there to make me smile or laugh, and even to lick away tears with sloppy kisses. I read a quote somewhere that said, "I wish I were as good a person as my dog thinks I am." Imagine how perfect the world would be if this were true. I know I will see you all up there again, one day, romping together in one happy pack. Because if dogs aren't in heaven . . . then it just wouldn't be heaven. I've loved and respected you all. Thank you for being my friends.

TIPS ON LIVING A STYLISH LIFE

On Knowing Who Is Alpha

When you have a pack like me, always greet the alpha first to avoid fights. In our house, that's Pasha, a poodle who is the smallest dog but who has the biggest personality.

On Eating Green

We like to buy a selection of treats for each size of pup. We also give canned organic green beans as a healthy option. You need to start them young on veggies, however, or they may not otherwise learn to like them.

▶ On Custom Creature Comforts

I like to have custom beds to match each room with custom monograms for the dogs. I use my own fabrics and Scotchgard them. However, the dogs also like to sleep in our bed.

On Soothing Nervous Travelers

When traveling with your pet, there is a special "doggie" Bach Rescue Remedy you can use to take the anxiety out of the trip. It can be purchased at Whole Foods.

▶ On Collars, Leashes, and Toys

The dogs adore their Swiss collars with brass cows on leather from Gstaad and their Anna Trzebinski collars from Africa. And the prettier the container, the better.

◀ On Being Covered

Slipcovers are a lifesaver if you allow your furry family on the sofas as we do. (Weekly dog baths help too.) My husband, Bernard, enjoys reading alongside Loretta.

A BELOVED
NEW YORK YORKIE

by Alex Papachristidis

Animals have always been a very important part of my life. When I was a child, I always took a Steiff stuffed animal with me wherever I went. My favorite childhood stories were all about animals — *The Tale of Squirrel Nutkin*, *Curious George*, *The Cat in the Hat*, *Winnie-the-Pooh*, and *The Travels of Babar*. I've had five dogs and a multitude of other pets over the years. This love of animals has also found its way into my interiors: I use print fabrics and carpets with such animal motifs as zebra stripes and integrate bronze and porcelain cats, turtles, monkeys, and elephant-shaped *objets*. In addition, birds and other animals often lurk in my custom-made Gracie Chinese wallpapers.

I love all animals, but our Yorkshire terrier, Teddy, is extra special. Teddy is much loved and pampered by my partner, Scott Nelson, a stylish accessories designer, and me — he is a most important part of our household. We share a country house with my sister, brother-in-law, and a niece and nephew and their spouses. Each has a dog, so Teddy has plenty of playmates. Teddy is treated like the Dauphin — nothing is too good for him. We adore him and take him everywhere we can. He travels the world like a gentleman, and is a calm and patient flyer. If we can't bring Teddy with us, we always miss him terribly.

Teddy has a very strong presence and character. He knows he is handsome — we call him the "Tom Cruise" of Yorkies — and he is always a ham for the camera. Teddy loves to be included in all of our activities, to frolic in our garden in the Hamptons, and to run freely on the beach.

Teddy loves lush interiors and enjoys them wherever he is. He is beautiful in an array of spaces, and appreciates craftsmanship and quality, whether he is lying on silk velvet or resting on an eighteenth-century daybed.

Teddy is the perfect pet for Scott and me — we can't imagine our lives without him. He is and always will be our beloved Theodore.

Theodore Nelson Papachristidis

NICKNAME: Teddy (#teddynewyorkie) AGE: 14 BREED: Yorkie
TEDDY'S HOMES: New York City and Bridgehampton

Interior designer and author Alex Papachristidis and accessories designer Scott Nelson share their homes with Teddy. Left and above: Teddy scampers across the New York City apartment's living room, and when it's time to go, he leaps into his Goyard travel bag.

TOP

Teddy's toys are kept neatly in a Majolica red shell container.

TIPS ON LIVING A STYLISH LIFE

◂ On Viewing His Kingdom

We take into account that Teddy loves to view his kingdom from above, by sitting on top of bed pillows or perching himself on the highest cushion on the back of sofas throughout our homes. We all prefer old-world fabrics—from silk to velvet—and are not concerned about Teddy's mishaps.

◂ On Forgiving Fabrics

Prints, patterns, and colors are the most forgiving when living with pets among beautiful things. For me, a Fortuny on the reverse that covers a sofa in the Hamptons house or a Schumacher ikat in our New York library are both attractive options that camouflage any of Teddy's accidents. Teddy likes to nap atop the apartment library sofa covered in a mélange of six different fabrics or lean in comfort on a silk velvet leopard Le Manach pillow.

▲ On Accessing Higher Ground

Small antique and vintage chairs next to beds and sofas help to give your pets access to higher ground while also protecting their backs. I often buy Teddy's miniature furniture from antiques stores, pier shows, and auction houses. I encourage my clients to do the same for their pets.

On Staying Fabulous

We work with a wonderful veterinarian, Bobete Gladstein, who practices both modern and holistic medicine and keeps Teddy healthy. She believes that as your dog ages, keeping him or her trim extends his or her life. Because of this, Teddy eats a special diet of home-cooked food, including tilapia, lean pork, or bison mixed with a variety of steamed vegetables, which keeps him slim and camera ready.

◀ On Creating Private Places

When designing my apartment, I reworked many of the spaces to adapt to our life with Teddy. One of my favorite features that we created is a small, mirrored, and stenciled niche to hide Teddy's Wee-Wee Pad. Teddy's private space is off the entrance hallway.

▼ On Collars, Leashes, and Travel Cases

Teddy has a choice of several collars and leashes that I keep organized in attractive trays. Teddy's favorite collar is his Goyard black and saddle, which matches his favorite Goyard travel bag. He also has other travel bags such as a Hermès purple leather bag.

▲ On Fur Versus Fashion

Teddy hates clothes. Even though we love bespoke suits
and pocket squares, for Teddy, his fur is good enough. But
being our son, of course, he does have all the classics—
custom-made Burberry rainwear, shearlings, and cashmere
sweaters. Teddy does like to bundle up in style when it gets
cold. I keep his clothes stored in an organized fashion in a
French gilt-metal-strapped chest of drawers with bronzed
lion's-paw feet.

▶ On Elevated Eats

The silver-plate tray Teddy eats from elevates his food.
I keep his food bowl (Blue Canton by Mottahedeh) and
rock-crystal water bowl on the tray. This arrangement looks
elegant and is comforting to Teddy.

A DACHSHUND'S TIMELESS STYLE

by Katie Ridder

What I've always looked for in a dog is what I've yet to find in a human being: unflinching loyalty, humble devotion, and the patience to follow me around and stare at me with loving eyes at any time of day or night—and have enough left over for my husband and children.

A love of dachshunds has always run in my family: my great-aunt Laura "Polly" Delano bred dachshunds for show, and Teddy came from a breeder who hoped he would join his mother at the Westminster Kennel Club Dog Show. Unfortunately for the breeder, Teddy exhibited a slight gap between his upper right incisor and the adjacent tooth. While we forgive Teddy for this imperfection (he seems unaware that he is anything short of a canine Adonis), this tooth issue and a slight inward turn on his front right paw put him out of competition. Remarkably placid for his breed, Teddy is unflappable and well-mannered. Rather than guard our house, Teddy welcomes visitors. He follows our friends around, able to discern which person is most likely to intuit his inner desires and give him the glorious scratch behind the ear or, better yet, the belly rub.

Although bred to seek small prey, Teddy is not a natural hunter. If he even bothers to chase a rabbit, he typically gives up after fifteen paces. His true love and the only subject on which he is a connoisseur is upholstered furniture. Teddy will turn up his nose at fifty/fifty Dacron/down cushions but feels totally at home on a one hundred-percent goose-down sofa. I would like to imagine that he has learned from his decorator owner but I believe his appreciation of comfort and fundamentally sweet nature come from within.

Teddy Pennoyer

AGE: 15 BREED: Dachshund TEDDY'S HOMES: Teddy lives in lower Westchester County and Millbrook, New York, and, during the month of August, Mishaum Point, Massachusetts.

ꬉꬉꬉ

Teddy shares his homes with interior designer
and author Katie Ridder, architect Peter Pennoyer,
and their three children, Jane, Tony, and Gigi.

ABOVE
A 1920s portrait of a dog named Snow hangs on
wallpaper from Katie's own collection in the entry hall.

RIGHT
In the living room, Teddy lounges on an
antique Oushak bought at auction.

ꬉꬉꬉꬉ

TIPS ON LIVING A STYLISH LIFE

On the Importance of a Luxe Faux Throw

One of my favorite pieces to include in a living room is a very luxe-looking faux-fur blanket. It looks great on a colored sofa and will also mask any dog hair.

◀ On Dirty Paws

An indoor/outdoor rug will endure any dirty paws or shedding coats. I especially love ones that have a sisal look but are made from polypropylene. You can scrub away accidents with soap and water without sacrificing the sophisticated look of the room.

On Collars

I don't wear high heels and Teddy doesn't wear a collar.

▲ On Down with Brown

I love to use throws in brown colorways as a bedcover. Teddy often hops onto our bed and the soft brown material hides his hair well. He enjoys sleeping on a fur that Susan Gutfreund gave Peter for his fiftieth birthday.

▶ On Feeling Secure

As Teddy has gotten older and increasingly more deaf, he's come to prefer a dog bed that encloses him—it seems to make him feel secure.

On Travel

When we travel to our weekend house, we bring Teddy's leash, toys, and treats in a tote bag customized with one of my fabrics.

MY DOGS: MY LIFE
by Carolyne Roehm

"You are the loves of my life and my soul's inspiration."

The above quote was written as a love song to another person but, while thinking of what to say about my beloved dogs (all six of them), the song sprang immediately into my mind. For indeed my pups, both past and present, inspire in me love, joy, passion, compassion, tenderness, and wonder. They bring forth the best in me.

My pups are astonishing individuals. All are different in breed, size, temperament, and personality. Their commonality is their love for me. I know this as surely as I know I exist. I have cuddle bears, great athletes, philosophers, old souls, pranksters, and gourmands. The largest and second oldest is a big baby who loves nothing more than playing in the mud or plunging into the snow, emerging with ice balls all over her coat. The tiniest (weighing in at 6.5 pounds) truly believes that she is a Great Dane–Doberman mix. They make me laugh with all their antics (and they can drive me crazy as well). I allow them to sit on every sofa and chair and most of the time some or all of them sleep with me. Things I would not easily forgive in a human—such as gnawing on the carved stretcher of a signed piece of eighteenth-century furniture (I know humans don't exactly do that but you get my drift)—I forgive in my dogs. I look into those sorry little eyes (yes, they know they have done a no-no), and all is forgotten. My mother always says, "Thank God you never had children, as they all would have been juvenile delinquents," as she gazes upon a roomful of shredded paper. We won't get into the fact that she is as smitten by them as I am.

Lucky	Beethoven	Trollop
AGE: 15 BREED: West Highland terrier	AGE: 5 BREED: Havanese	AGE: 4 BREED: Australian Kelpie
Dusty	**Baby Monkey**	**Teddy Bear**
AGE: 10 BREED: Havanese	AGE: 5 BREED: Havanese	AGE: 9 BREED: Wheaten terrier

THE SIX PUPS' HOME: Weatherstone in Sharon, Connecticut

Yes, these beautiful creatures make me laugh and fill my heart with joy. But, as all dog lovers know, these special spirits can also break your heart. When we lose them through an accident, illness, or old age, we are consumed with grief and a pain that is intolerable. We lose a giant piece of our hearts and our spirits. When I lost a beloved pup, I felt as if I wanted to die. I recall saying, "Please don't leave me behind—I cannot live without you." Just to think about this sad inevitability brings tears to my eyes.

My sustaining hope is that when I am no longer meant for this world, I will come to my special place in the universe to rest. There I shall find that the grass is green, with a few glorious trees for shade, some beautiful and sweetly scented flowers, and a small, cool trickling brook. All of my loves will be there happily romping and running blissfully around me. I shall spend an eternity caressing their soft ears, rubbing all those tummies, and gazing into all of their loving eyes. To live forever after with them is my dream and prayer.

Designer and author Carolyne Roehm and occasionally her companion, Simon Pinniger, share her home with her six pups.

ABOVE, LEFT
Baby Monkey's favorite perch when not on Carolyne's lap is an eighteenth-century Italian painted chair, covered in an embroidered Chelsea Editions fabric.

OPPOSITE
Carolyne and some of the dogs stroll through the living room.

ABOVE

In the stair hall is one of a pair of terra-cotta dog statues, circa late eighteenth century. Carolyne bought these years ago in San Francisco when she gave a talk on her book *A Passion for Blue & White*.

RIGHT

Carolyne's "babies" love to be up high in the reading/television room in front of the big fireplace. She keeps plenty of dog blankets on hand to cover the sofa. The marble bust of an emperor is nineteenth century.

TIPS ON LIVING A STYLISH LIFE

◄ On Dog Covers: Vive la France

Over twenty years ago I learned from a French woman selling high-end textiles in her Parisian shop about a fabulous idea for a dog cover to protect my furniture: Buy extra yardage of a fabric that you are using to upholster sofas and chairs to make matching dog covers. The covers will blend in with the upholstery and when they get dirty, you can send them to the dry cleaners. I lightly quilt the fabric covers and dress them up with a pretty trim. Alternatively, you can also quilt a cover, turn it, and not add trim, which makes it practically disappear atop your upholstered furniture.

On Clothes and Collars

Dusty has a favorite red holiday sweater; Lucky has a genuine Loden coat; Trollop has a Burberry raincoat; Teddy has a ThunderShirt, as she gets nervous; while Beethoven and Baby Monkey have matching black-and-white houndstooth-check jackets. My country dogs shed their collars by rolling in the Canadian goose dung on the property every time I put them on.

► On Winter Days and Entryways

In the wintertime, I keep a basket of towels that look good, color-wise, by the door where I can easily catch a pup when he or she races into the house covered with snow or rain or has muddy feet.

▲ On Creating Dog-Friendly Human Beds

I do sleep with my pups. All have their own special spot on my canopy bed—one on my head, one on my feet, one on a down pillow, one on a nearby bench, one behind my knees so she can't turn over, and one underneath the bed. I protect my bed by making a dog cover (see "On Dog Covers: Vive la France") in the same fabric as my bedding or find a coordinating lightweight fleece. The dog cover works visually and keeps my sheets somewhat clean.

On Water Breaks that Won't Break the Floor

I place a mat under my water bowls, as I have some sloppy drinkers. I have ruined a couple of wooden floors without them, and I find that this solution helps.

REFLECTIONS ON TRICKY, MY EXTRAORDINARY HOUND

by Schuyler Samperton

One balmy night in early June
My neighbor rang me up:
"I found a dog! You're going to swoon!"
That's how I met my pup . . .

I wasn't looking for a pooch,
But oh, that little face!
He won me over with a smooch
And fuzzy-pawed embrace.

Intrepid at but four months old,
A parking lot he'd roam.
His rescuer was adamant—
I had to take him home!

I named him Tricky
(Not because his temperament was rough),
And soon we were inseparable,
I couldn't get enough.

Now anyone who knows me knows
He's always close at hand.
I take him with me everywhere.
We've traveled 'cross the land.

He's chased the squirrels of Central Park,
And sailed the coast of Maine.
He's gone antiquing in Palm Beach
And never did complain.

He's at my feet and patient
When I try to learn guitar,
And fusses not when I insist
On singing in the car.

He's been my one true constant light
When push turns into shove.
He's sat beside me when I've said
Good-bye to those I've loved.

You'll always be my best, best friend,
My snuggly little guy.
You make my life so wonderful!
How fortunate am I?

Tricky

AGE: 9 **BREED:** Sheepdog-terrier mix
TRICKY'S HOMES: Los Angeles, Florida, and an island off the coast of Maine

Interior designer Schuyler Samperton and her companion, Marc Lazard, share their homes with Tricky. Above: Schuyler serenades Tricky in the Los Angeles living room.

RIGHT
Nothing says gravitas like dog portraiture. An oil painting of your best friend is bound to be a most treasured possession and a future family heirloom.

FAR RIGHT
Schuyler protects Tricky's favorite snuggly spot with layered, washable throws. Prints and textures help to hide paw prints while lending a louche, bohemian air to upholstered pieces.

TIPS ON LIVING A STYLISH LIFE

◀ On No Limits and Linens

Since nothing is off-limits to Tricky, I'm a big believer in using outdoor fabrics on upholstery. Rough n' Rowdy by Perennials is my favorite: it looks like a lovely, thick-weight linen. We even have a bright white sofa covered in it in Florida, and it's perfect. Needless to say, washable throws are fabulous—I use them on sofas and beds and am particularly fond of any type of exotic, colorful print.

▶ On Being Stylishly Sentimental

It's always nice to be greeted by the real thing, but a soulful photo of your pooch on an entrance table is also a good substitute—especially when combined with some of your favorite objects.

On Collars, Leashes, and Clothes

I'm a huge fan of collars by Henry Beguelin and Calleen Cordero. I love how the embroidered leather and brass pops against Tricky's fur. I don't normally do outfits, but I have been known to dress Tricky up in a reversible red-and-black plaid Filson coat when the temperature dips below freezing.

▼ On Favorite Places to Sleep

Tricky loves to sleep next to me.

A SOUTHERN FRENCH BULLDOG AT HOME

by Mark D. Sikes

Lily came to us from Atlanta. We like to think of her as our Georgia Peach. She is very much a Southern lady in many ways: soft-spoken and delicate, with a special charm. Not to mention she is, of course, adorable. And like every parent, I am totally objective about that. (No, really, we can't leave the house without strangers affirming this fact.)

All this is true until she is crossed and then—look out. Lily doesn't like loud noises, strangers, or car rides, and she makes this very clear. She is an excellent guard dog—all twelve pounds of her.

We did not know it at the time, but when Lily arrived in California she was quite sick. Like many French bulldogs, she suffered from serious breathing complications and had to endure many surgeries. Many a night we have sat up with an oxygen machine nursing her back to health. Eight years later, she is doing great and seems to have more spunk now than she did years ago. Of course, she takes full advantage of her earlier troubles, and gets away with murder regularly. I like to say our house is really Lily's house and she just lets us live there too. In fact, due to the way she expects to be treated, Lily has earned quite the nickname: "HRH," as in "Her Royal Highness."

Lily has brought so much joy and laughter into our house. (Or is it her house?) It's hard to think of life without her. When she is gone on occasion, it just isn't the same. Like a true Southern lady, she knows how to make an entrance and fill a room with her unique charms.

We love you, Lily.

Lily (also known as HRH Lily)

AGE: 9 BREED: French bulldog

LILY'S HOME: Hollywood Hills, California

‍‍‍‍ℓℓℓℓℓ

Interior designer and author Mark D. Sikes and his partner, Michael Griffin, share their Hollywood Hills home with Lily. Opposite: Here, Lily enjoys guarding the front door.

ABOVE

Lily coordinates well with the neutral living room palette. The shells and coral in the fireplace were collected on travels, and bought at curiosity stores or on eBay. The natural fiber rug is durable against paw traffic.

RIGHT

Lily sits on a daybed covered in Carolina Irving's Patmos Stripe, her favorite spot to take naps.

‍‍‍‍ℓℓℓℓℓ

OPPOSITE

Lily loves how Mark redid this room just off the garden in shades of greens and blues. The doors are always open to the outside. Because Lily slips on the hardwood floors, there are lots of rugs in her path, including this antique dhurrie.

ABOVE

The terraced backyard has steps up the middle that lead to different landing areas planted with boxwood or hydrangea; the brick walls are covered in fig ivy. Lily doesn't like going up the steps but with a little help she usually cooperates.

TIPS ON LIVING A STYLISH LIFE

On Cashmere and the Cleaners

We often throw a cashmere blanket on top of the sofa before Lily gets on it. Not only does the blanket protect the sofa, but she also adores it. We send it to the cleaners as need be.

▶ On Collars, Leashes, and Clothes

Since Lily has breathing issues, she does not wear a collar. When she goes on walks, we use a harness. She has several of them in lots of colors with matching leashes. When the weather is cold, we dress up Lily in a cashmere cable-knit sweater. Lily doesn't get to wear it in L.A. very often.

▶ On Finicky Eaters

Since Lily is such a picky eater and not a fan of dog food, we make her food fresh every day: three kinds of meat, such as steak and liver, mixed with carrots and peas and other vegetables. Unfortunately, she doesn't like leftovers, and sometimes she will spit out the peas.

▲ On Favorite Places to Sleep

Lily likes to sleep in the middle of our bed under the covers with her head on a pillow.

For dog beds, we like to match each to the rug in the room so they are coordinated.

BIG SUR AND BIG LOVE IN THE SANTA MONICA HILLS

by Windsor Smith

To Sur with love: The sound of his name signifies respect. But spell it out and you'll learn that our dark, dapper "Sur" is named for Big Sur. Not because he's a large dog—which he clearly is—but because opening our hearts to the raw energy of this remarkable puppy has all the peaks and hidden wellsprings of that rugged, awesomely beautiful stretch of coastline.

No surprise, then, how much Sur grooves on riding shotgun up and down the Pacific Coast Highway in my husband's '66 convertible Corvette. Sometimes when I see those two going on yet another adventure, I think they were brothers in a previous life, maybe even twins. Both are dark, statuesque, clever, and loyal, with still waters that run amazingly wide and deep.

It took us six and a half years to even begin to think about opening our home to another puppy after losing Zona, the female shepherd who served as companion, protector, and healer of our children, now grown. She was elegant, spiritual, and in many ways an archive of our lives. Then in walks this big, lumbering male dog whose previous rogue manners had been instilled by his being mascot of a college fraternity house. He's king of our tennis court and lives to catch a fly ball, a rebound shot, or a high lob. Yet he's also gentle, witty, and intuitive: with one cock of those giant ears, he can size up any situation. He's elegant company who adores unconditionally. And he taught us to do just that all over again, with his persistence and his nudging nose. We fell deep.

Sur

AGE: 2 BREED: German shepherd
SUR'S HOME: Santa Monica Hills, California

Interior designer and author Windsor Smith, her husband, Anthony Buttino, a real estate developer, and their children, Oliver and Trinity, share with Sur their well-appointed home, just 6,793 steps from the beach and 2,543 steps from their favorite hiking path through the Santa Monica Hills.

LEFT
Sur loves to sit vigil in the front entry hall not only to officiate the comings and goings of the house, but also because the Thassos and Atlas gray stone keeps him cool on a hot summer day.

OPPOSITE
Ralph Lauren's bone-black high-gloss paint in the "great room" woodwork is no match for Sur's shiny black coat.

TIPS ON LIVING
A STYLISH LIFE

On L.A. Lounging

As an L.A. dog with a shepherd's coat, our Sur is content lounging on the cool kitchen floor, although he enjoys his bamboo dog bed too. For families where canines share the sofa, I'd be mindful of using durable, high-performance, stain-repellant fabrics. That's easy to do since outdoor textiles have become so luxurious in look and feel—including an outdoor weave that's a dead ringer for cashmere.

On Being "Professional Sur"

Training is everything. It doesn't hurt that we have one of the smartest dog species on the planet, but dogs do very well with structure and repetition, as well as consistency. We've designated certain areas of the house for specific activities and, believe it or not, Sur responds with a very different composure in the living room than in the kitchen or mudroom, where he's free to get his dog on by dribbling a tennis ball or chomping on a marrow bone. In the living room, he's our super-composed "Professorial Sur." We've found that establishing the game rules early on is a win-win for our family, for our furnishings, and especially for our dog, who appreciates the structure.

On Collars and Clothes

Bottega Veneta collars are divine—I'm a sucker for *intrecciato* weaves. As for clothes, Sur is not shy. So, it's *au naturel* for him.

LAB LOVE IN MALIBU

by Nathan Turner and Eric Hughes

When Nacho was a puppy, our good pal Mary McDonald (a.k.a. Mums) declared him the supermodel of Labrador retrievers: a perfect physical specimen—but maybe not the brightest star in the galaxy. We soon discovered Nacho had his own special skill set: He might not be book smart but he sure was beach smart. He's the ultimate athlete and there's not another Lab out there who can ride a wave like Nacho. He's the happiest dude on our beach and is friends with everyone, even the occasional seal.

Nacho really came into his own at the beach and we can't imagine life in Malibu without him. He's our partner in crime for everything fun, as we all love body surfing and hiking the hills, and we also appreciate ending any activity with an afternoon nap. And not to mention—like us—he is always up for a snack.

Recently Wallace Eugene (a.k.a. Wally) came along, our third-generation Lab. A spirited puppy who refused to be crate trained . . . oh joy. Our trainer had advised us to let him cry and eventually he'd stop but boy, did she get it wrong, because every time he was put in the crate he would wail. Finally, Nacho, with a worried brow, sat right in front of his crate until Wally's crying slowed to silence. That was the beginning of their bond and they've been best pals ever since: such happy, dopey brothers. Nacho has since helped Wally navigate beach life, from how to get beyond the break to the art of chasing seagulls.

Life with these two rascals is a wonder, and we are so happy and proud these pups chose us. We love this quote by the wonderful Roger Caras (author, television and radio personality, and animal activist): "Dogs are not our whole lives, but they make our lives whole."

Nacho
AGE: 8 BREED: Labrador retriever

Wallace Eugene (a.k.a. Wally)
AGE: 2 BREED: Labrador retriever

NACHO AND WALLY'S HOMES: During the week in a Beverly Hills mid-century modern apartment. Weekends are spent in a little place in Malibu (on Dog Beach).

Interior designer, chef, and author Nathan Turner and interior designer Eric Hughes
share their homes with Nacho and Wally. The dogs spend weekdays at Nathan and Eric's
design office. Left: Nacho and Willy pose for the camera while relaxing on a protective
utility canvas blanket, which is invaluable at a home by the sea and when traveling.

ABOVE

Nacho striking a patriotic pose in front of the abstract flag photograph by Oberto Gili.
His dog bed is covered in a blue-and-white paisley-inspired pattern.

꩜

ABOVE

Gouache drawings of Nathan and Eric's late dog, Daisy, and Nacho
by Vanessa Martin adorn the wall.

OPPOSITE

Since they never met a stripe they didn't like, Eric had blue and white
stripes painted everywhere outside.

꩜

ABOVE
Sunbrella fabric is used for Nacho and Wally's
bed; it is resistant to almost everything.

RIGHT
A gift from Eric to Nathan: a framed collar
of their late, beloved dog, Daisy.

TIPS ON LIVING A STYLISH LIFE

▶ On Getting Hooked

For incredibly active dogs and their humans, make sure to have plenty of hooks right by the doorway, especially assigned for leashes, extra collars, and play paraphernalia. Nacho and Wally have lots of collars. Our favorite right now is by Found My Animal. It's a natural rope collar with red leather closures. The dogs' beach collars are super cool too—they are bright orange, waterproof, and from L. L. Bean.

◀ On Throwing Shade

If you love to take your dogs to the beach like we do, make sure to bring an extra umbrella for them for sun protection.

▶ On Staying Cool and Clean

We use a large galvanized tub for water and just keep it out on the porch. It's ideal for big dogs.

On Keeping Character

We like keeping the dogs' toys in containers that have character. No need for plastic when a vintage tin will do.

THE WONDERFUL WORLD OF WILLIE

by Kelly Wearstler

When I first saw Willie, he was wearing a pink cable-knit sweater vest. With his tail wagging, he caught my attention with his sweet, soulful, dark eyes. He looked deeply at me as if he were thinking, *I feel like I've known you my whole life*. I couldn't resist. We just had to bring him home.

Meeting Willie was an unexpected treasure. We were hosting an event for Best Friends Animal Society three years ago at my store in West Hollywood. A few days before the event they called asking if they could bring along some dogs that were in need of adoption. The next thing you know, Willie arrives at my door in a big Best Friend's double-decker bus.

Willie is always happy—his tail is perpetually wagging. He follows me around in the morning when I'm getting ready for my day and sometimes comes to the studio with me and rests in my lap while I'm sketching and taking meetings. He's a great listener and appreciative in his own way, giving kisses with abandon at any and every moment.

When we fell in love with Willie, we thought we'd give him a new name. He had been adopted previously and then returned to the shelter. New beginning, new family, new name, perhaps? Yet as we got to know him, we knew he was forever Willie. He's our L'il Will, curious and loving and always at the ready to join in the family fun. When he's tired, he gets a little snappy and then he's our Will Pill. No matter his mood, we realized he is truly a Willie inside and out.

Willie

AGE: 3½ BREED: Gray and white terrier scruff-daddy mix WILLIE'S HOMES: Willie likes to mix things up by going between our home in Beverly Hills and our pad in Malibu on the weekends, which he considers pretty cool.

Interior designer and author Kelly Wearstler, her husband, hotelier Brad Korzen, and their sons, Oliver and Elliott, share their homes with Willie. Opposite: Willie enjoys soaking in the sun on the teak deck at the beach house, which is surrounded by a frameless glass railing. The house's pickled cedar wood paneling is punctuated with copper and blackened metal up-lit sconces. A rock, peeking out of the ocean at low tide, is the visual centerpiece.

ABOVE

The user-friendly fabrics throughout the beach house are textured. The patinated leathers, like the chair Willie is standing on, along with the shaggy carpeting are extremely forgiving too.

The furniture throughout the beach house is low-slung, making it
easily reachable for Willie. Relaxed and easy-to-wash coverlets are
draped on the beds just in case he picks up dirt before chilling out.

TIPS ON LIVING A STYLISH LIFE

◀ On Helping Them Stay Off the Furniture

Having soft and cozy beds for your dogs to lounge in helps to keep them off furniture. We created a collection of cushy, stylish beds with high-performance fabrics; they're eco-friendly and have hypoallergenic filling. I have a few at home and in the studio for whenever Willie visits.

▶ On Not Getting Pushed Around

Whenever Willie would drink water from his old bowl, he would push it across the floor, the bowl scratching it and spilling water everywhere along the way. This inspired me to design a set of marble dog bowls that not only are luxurious; they can't be easily pushed.

▶ On Collars

I designed these super-luxe black leather collars with burnished bronze tags. They can be engraved with your dog's name and your contact information.

BARKÉ DIEM WITH PIPER AND KIPPY

by Hutton Wilkinson

Our pups, Piper Dundee and Kippy of the Cavendish, are brother and sister, and they follow in the paw prints of their two late older brothers, Jip and Argyle.

Piper came first, as he is one year older than his sister, and he ruled the castle as the heir apparent and lord of the manor for one short year before being dethroned by his upstart sister. To say that he was pleased with his change in stature would be a lie, and we still have the stained carpets to prove it. Piper is a loving, stubborn, sweet, noncombative sort of guy. He is extremely handsome and no one knows that more than he does. Piper is what I like to call "faithful, not fawning."

Kippy was named after a little dog who used to live at Rosa Lewis's Cavendish Hotel in London. Kippy is the exact opposite of her brother and most likely less "to the manor born" than her namesake. She is bossy yet obedient, as well as devious, cunning, and not always honest, although we can never prove if she "did it" . . . or if Piper "did it." It's gotten to the point now that I just tell Ruth that "I did it," which for some strange reason, actually makes sense to her.

Kippy has a way of getting Piper's treat and eating it too. She's definitely one of those gals who thinks "what's hers is hers and what's his is hers." Kippy doesn't think she's as beautiful as she should be, so we spend an awful lot of time telling her how pretty she is, and at this point she actually believes it—although her behavior doesn't reflect her newfound loveliness.

Together these two can get into a lot of mischief, and for two parents who are accustomed to having only one baby at a time, this new arrangement sometimes seems like too much. We miss not being able to take them to parties and openings as we did with our boy Jip, who was invited everywhere and regularly written up in the columns.

Piper Dundee

AGE: 9 BREED: West Highland white terrier

Kippy of the Cavendish

AGE: 8 BREED: West Highland white terrier

PIPER AND KIPPY'S HOMES: They live in Casa la Condessa, a house in Beverly Hills, California, which is part of the Dawnridge estate. Weekends are spent at La Finca Alastaya, a house in Malibu.

And we regret not being able to take them with us when we travel, as we did with Argyle, who was a joyous handful. Just the thought of wrangling these two rascals onto a jet is too daunting a thought for us to even consider.

So we have two lovely stay-at-home pups, happy to be with us whenever we're around, and that's all we care about. Thank God they're not writing this about us . . . we can only imagine what they would have to say about our habits.

Interior designer and author Hutton Wilkinson and his wife, Ruth, share their homes with Piper and Kippy. According to the dogs, "They are the *conde y condessa de Alastaya.*" Above: Here, at the foot of the stairs in front of a mural of Venice, they share time with Ruth.

RIGHT
Piper and Kippy love to bound down the majestic staircase.

ꙮ

LEFT

Piper and Kippy love their leopard carpet because it's the only one in the house they can really make a mess of and not get caught. Leopard is the most dog-friendly pattern in the world—Hutton and Ruth credit designer Elsie de Wolfe and her beloved poodles for discovering how forgiving it is.

BOTTOM, LEFT

A carved coral Westie and porcelain pug crown jewelry boxes in Ruth's dressing room. The antique blue "japanned" box is from the collection of Elsie de Wolfe. The "gilded" eggs and boxes were hand-painted for Ruth by Hutton.

ABOVE

Piper and Kippy are proud of their ancestral crest with its crenelated and turreted Scottish castle and their illustrious crossed-dog-bone emblem.

OPPOSITE

The needlepoint pillows are from Ruth's Westie memorabilia collection. The pillow on the right was a gift from an English friend; the one on the left was created by Ruth in memory of her first Westie, Jip.

ꙮ

TIPS ON LIVING A STYLISH LIFE

On Our House Policy

My policy is to mess up the house as fast as possible so that I can redecorate. Piper and Kippy do their best to accommodate me. And what they don't do, I do by putting my shoes on the furniture, as I believe in "live and let live"—and that goes for dogs as well. What happens, happens. We have no rules about who can and can't sit on the furniture and get comfortable.

On Collars and Clothes

The dogs wear practical collars every day. Ruth made a fancy blue-and-green plaid petit point collar with a soft backing for Piper and a pink-and-green plaid one for Kippy for special occasions. When the dogs help us out in hosting cocktail and dinner parties, Kippy gets to wear a pink taffeta ribbon and Piper wears a blue taffeta ribbon, and bows. Our dogs are basically nudists and put up with the formalities of a collar.

On Grooming

Piper and Kippy love to go to the hairdresser all the time because they have a lot of fun there. However, no matter how hard they try, they can't seem to get dirty enough to encourage us to take them more often.

On Luxurious Snoozes and Snoring

They eat out of bowls fit for a roadside diner; however, they do have
a glamorous dog bed, which was a gift from their pal Chad Holman,
president of the silk company Jim Thompson Fabrics. It's all stitched
up with brilliantly woven brocades in orange and pinks. Out at the
ranch they have a Chippendale Chinese bed that matches our own
nineteenth-century one. Even so, they still prefer to sleep on top of
our heads and make our lives miserable in the middle of the night by
snoring and generally kicking us out of bed entirely.

On Scottish Snacks

We serve Kippy and Piper solid-gold health food. For a special
treat, Ruth makes them homemade peanut butter biscuits,
gingerbread, or white-chocolate biscotti. The dogs like when we
are away because their sitter gives them imported shortbread treats
from Scotland, sent by their friend Benji's parents. The shortbread
helps them to stay connected to their Scottish heritage.

A LOVE AFFAIR WITH A DOG (OR TWO)

by Bunny Williams

After losing our beloved whippet Elizabeth and seeing our adorable terrier mix Lucy move into old age, it seemed the right time to add to the pack. Nights spent on my favorite website, PetFinder.com, finally produced a picture of a face with eyes that haunted me. With a click of the mouse, I found that Annabelle (her given name was Kaylee) was in Bulverde, Texas. I was so lucky that my friend Lisa Kopecky lived near the shelter where she was being cared for. She was able to arrange the adoption, and the next day tucked Annabelle into a bag, put her under the seat on the airplane, and brought her to New York. We met her at the Lowell Hotel, and it was love at first sight for the three of us—John and I bonded with her immediately, as she did with us. We then gave her a new name—Annabelle. From the first moment, she became our shadow. She loves her walks in the city but it is in the country where she is the most happy. I think there is still a lot of cowgirl in her. Whether chasing squirrels or jumping in the pool or the garden troughs (she must be part water dog), she is in ecstasy. However, she is never far from either of us. Her favorite time is running through the water from a hose when we are watering the flowerpots. But in the house, she is in our laps or next to our chairs. Those eyes stare at us and we cannot believe how lucky we are to have her.

After losing Lucy, it was time to find a friend for Annabelle. Back to PetFinder.com, and again there appeared another tiny face with big eyes. In this case, before we could adopt her, there were four personal interviews with friends and a site visit to our home to see if we would be acceptable owners. Luckily, we passed and on a Friday evening two dear girls arrived with this tiny, fluffy, skinny thing. I fell in love immediately but John was a bit skeptical of this shy, scared little creature. He agreed, reluctantly I think, that she could stay. Little by little this tiny white fluff ball, whom we named Bebe, filled out and now resembles Phyllis Diller and is the ruler of the house. During the day, she is completely independent, disappearing to hunt chipmunks and chase birds, but at night she is in our laps begging for love and kisses. One of my favorite sights is when I'm driving to the country and I look over and see John asleep with Bebe napping on his chest.

The pleasure our dogs bring us cannot be measured.

Annabelle
AGE: 6
BREED: Terrier mix

Bebe
AGE: 3½ BREED: Terrier
and poodle mix

ANNABELLE AND BEBE'S HOMES: Annabelle and Bebe live in Falls Village, Connecticut, on weekends and in Manhattan during the week.

Interior designer and author Bunny Williams and antiques dealer John Rosselli share their homes with Annabelle and Bebe. Left: The faux leopard carpet is very forgiving for little doggie paws. It also keeps Annabelle from slipping down the stairs.

BELOW
Bunny and Annabelle stroll through the sunken garden of the Connecticut retreat.

OPPOSITE
One of Bebe's jobs is to test the guest room bed before visitors arrive to make sure it is comfortable.

𝓮𝓵𝓵𝓮

ABOVE

Indian-quilted spreads tucked around sofa cushions make the dogs feel as much at home
as their humans. They also have their own dog beds everywhere.

OPPOSITE

Old pine floorboards in the entrance hall were stenciled with an ancient geometric pattern
resembling a tortoise shell. Annabelle loves bounding through this hall on her way to bed.

TIPS ON LIVING A STYLISH LIFE

◄ On Matching Coverage

Cover sofa cushions with throws
or quilts that match the furniture.
Faux-fur throws look chic in winter.
All should be washed regularly.

▼ On Knowing
Your Limits

Limit the area where the dogs enter
the house, and in this space have a
supply of towels in a basket, along
with brushes.

▶ On Putting a Dog Bed in Your Favorite Rooms

Put dog beds under the tables in rooms where you spend the most time. I love the faux-leopard WallyBed, as do the dogs; these beds look good in any space and are extremely practical. Annabelle and Bebe's other favorite place to sleep is on our beds, but there isn't much room for them.

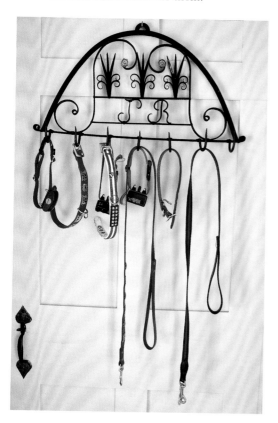

▲ On Collars and Clothes

Annabelle and Bebe wear red leather collars, with their names and phone numbers on chips. They are outfitted in red fleece-lined parkas during the winter months.

▶ On Offering Refreshment

After chasing chipmunks and rabbits, the dogs are thirsty, so a full water bowl always awaits. The raffia bone is the placemat for their food bowls.

IT'S A DOG'S LIFE

Jonathan Adler's FOXYLADY

HOW I CAME INTO JONATHAN AND SIMON'S LIFE: I was found at the North Shore Animal League shelter. I just flashed my cute face and sassy tail plumage—they couldn't resist. FAVORITE PLACE I AM NOT SUPPOSED TO BE: Underfoot. But I just can't help myself. MOST TROUBLE I'VE EVER GOTTEN IN: I once ate a bottle of prescription pills and had to get my stomach pumped. It was very Young Hollywood. MY GUILTY PLEASURE: Admiring the Mimi Vang Olsen's portrait of *moi* that hangs in Jonny and Simon's bedroom. SPECIAL TALENT: Resting bitch face. FAVORITE PLACE TO WALK: Washington Square Park with my guys. PET PEEVE: When I get brought to Jonathan's "Fantasy Factory" headquarters in Soho. So. Much. Manhandling.

Martyn Lawrence Bullard's DAISY

HOW I CAME INTO MARTYN AND MICHAEL'S LIFE: They found me in a daisy field in Dallas. FAVORITE PLACE I AM NOT SUPPOSED TO BE: I like to hide in my daddies' shower on the cold marble, especially when I've stolen a sock to chew on. FAVORITE MEAL AT HOME: Lamb chops . . . off the bone, of course. FAVORITE RESTAURANT AND WHAT I ORDER: A big lump of Brie at Farm, a French bistro in Palm Springs. MOST TROUBLE I'VE EVER GOTTEN IN: I'm perfect. Ask my daddies. MY GUILTY PLEASURE: Mozzarella string cheese sticks from Trader Joe's. SPECIAL TALENT: Peekaboo tricks. FAVOR-ITE PLACE TO SLEEP: On the bed between my two daddies. FAVORITE PLACE TO WALK: Around our hillside at sunset with my daddy Michael. PET PEEVE: I don't like wearing my doggy booties when the ground is too hot . . . even though they do give some amazing "runway" style to my walk.

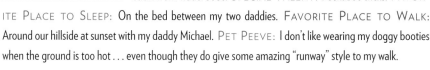

OPPOSITE
One of FoxyLady's roommates is this faux poodle, which was
a gift to Simon Doonan from designer Michael Kors.

Betsy Burnham's LOLA, NINA GARCIA, and FELIX

HOW WE CAME INTO BETSY, MARK, CARSON, AND WILL'S LIFE: We (Lola and Nina) came from breeders, respectively from the Southeast and Chicago. I (Felix) came through the Los Angeles–based rescue group Wags and Walks. When I was picked up from the Carson/Gardena Animal Care Center in Gardena, California, I was in pretty bad shape. As a foster for Wags, Betsy was working to find a forever home for me but once groomed, I was so adorable that at a point when I was on my best behavior, the family decided to keep me. Now Wags calls Betsy a "foster fail," but I feel as if I won the lottery. FAVORITE PLACE WE ARE NOT SUPPOSED TO BE: I (Lola) like hanging out the driver's side window of Betsy's car, balanced on her arm. I'm not supposed to be there as it's dangerous for her to drive like that. I (Nina) enjoy hanging out atop any table. I once ate an entire turkey sandwich on the breakfast table when no one was looking. I (Felix) like digging up flowerbeds in the backyard. MOST TROUBLE WE'VE EVER GOTTEN IN: I (Lola) wasn't getting enough attention at Christmas so I walked across the living room's seagrass rug and peed on it. Betsy was so furious and ended up buying a gate for the room's doorway; now we can't go into the room. By the way, seagrass doesn't clean up very easily. See my (Nina's) story about turkey sandwich above. When I (Felix) first moved into our house, I lifted my leg inside. That wasn't good. OUR FAVORITE OUTFIT: No way, José. OUR GUILTY PLEASURES: I (Lola) get acupuncture every five weeks or so. It's fabulous. I (Nina) love cat food. PET PEEVE: I (Lola) can't stand Felix. He's literally ruined my life. When I (Nina) see the suitcases come out, I start shaking. Betsy bought me this dog "anxiety coat" that they put on me to make me feel secure during scary times, and it actually helps. Wet grass in the morning bums me (Felix) out. Otherwise, I'm pretty chill.

Robert Couturier's HERCULE, CLARA, ZAZOU, and DORA

HOW WE CAME INTO ROBERT AND JEFFREY'S LIFE: I (Hercule) come from a very elegant breeder—I am a champion dog and black, which is very rare. FAVORITE PLACE I AM NOT SUPPOSED TO BE: In the downstairs living room. I don't know why, but I like to drop a little smelly present there. FAVORITE RESTAURANT AND WHAT I ORDER: Ridiculous—I don't eat out. FAVORITE MEAL AT HOME: I eat chicken, duck, rice, and vegetables cooked fresh every day. FAVORITE PLACE TO SLEEP: In my daddies' bed. MOST TROUBLE I'VE EVER GOTTEN IN: I don't get into trouble—I am perfect. SPECIAL TALENT: I don't need a special talent as I am loveable just as I am, just being me. FAVORITE PLACE TO WALK: Walking around the gardens on our property and taking walks in the countryside with my daddies. PET PEEVE: Noise—any sort of discordant noise makes me crazy.

Steven Gambrel's SAILOR

HOW I CAME INTO STEVEN AND JAMES'S LIFE: My parents met my handsome cousin Hobie through their friends in Sag Harbor—and the rest is history. FAVORITE PLACE I AM NOT SUPPOSED TO BE: There are places I'm not supposed to be? FAVORITE PLACE TO SLEEP: In my dads' bed. FAVORITE RESTAURANT AND WHAT I ORDER: The Hunter's Head Tavern in Upperville, Virginia, when I am visiting my grandparents. I order the Furry Foody (organic raw beef and sweet potato). I also like Salt on Shelter Island—the hamburgers are delicious. FAVORITE MEAL AT HOME: Scrambled eggs with spinach. MOST TROUBLE I'VE EVER GOTTEN IN: I've never been in trouble—I don't know what that is. MY GUILTY PLEASURE: Lying on feathery down pillows in my dads' bed or on their heads, if they stay still long enough. SPECIAL TALENT: With all my swimming and running, my parents think I'm a fantastic athlete. I learned to swim by hanging on to my cousin Isaac's tail while he swam around Upper Sag Harbor Cove. FAVORITE PLACE TO WALK: The spectacular ocean beaches with my parents and grandparents. I get super excited and begin to squeal as soon as I smell the salt air. PET PEEVE: I get so terribly disappointed when the local bar runs out of dog treats. They almost always have a container of yumminess waiting for the neighborhood pups.

Brooke Giannetti's BEBE, FRASIER, SERA, and SOPHIE

HOW WE CAME INTO THE GIANNETTI FAMILY'S LIFE: Frasier and Bebe were already in the Giannetti family when upholsterer Sherry Alfaro introduced them to breeder Tammy Dekel of the Shih Tzu Station. Brooke and Steve fell in love with me (Sophie) and brought me home. A year later, Tammy called Brooke to let her know that Sera, my half sister, needed a home too. Brooke likes to tell people that she and Steve have "two pairs" of pups: she thinks it sounds less crazy than having four dogs. FAVORITE PLACE WE ARE NOT SUPPOSED TO BE: Whenever Brooke can't find us, she knows that we are curled up on Nick's bed, waiting for him to come home from college. FAVORITE MEAL AT HOME: When Brooke serves us a bowl of delicious PureVita. FAVORITE MEAL OUT: We like Azu in Ojai. Since we don't over-order, Steve occasionally drops some tasty chicken in our bowls; Brooke pretends not to notice. FAVORITE OUTFIT: We like to show off our naturally flowing, long fur, so no adornment is needed for us. MOST TROUBLE WE'VE EVER GOTTEN IN: We are too cute to get into too much trouble, although Brooke is not happy when we eat goat poo on the farm. We can't help ourselves—it's delicious and looks just like chocolate chips. OUR GUILTY PLEASURE: Brooke takes us for a day of beauty every Thursday. We get a blowout and look fabulous for about twenty-four hours. Then one of us throws up. FAVORITE PLACE TO WALK: We love our outings in town, especially visiting the ladies at the local department store, Rains. They give us treats and rub our tummies. PET PEEVE: The three goats on the farm: Thelma, Louise, and Dot. Every time we try to play with them, they butt us in the head.

Brian J. McCarthy's DAISY

HOW I CAME INTO BRIAN AND DANNY'S LIFE: Have a Heart Animal Welfare Fund had signed me up on Facebook, and that's how Brian and Danny discovered me. They stalked my Facebook page while I studied their Facebook page full of photos of their homes. Once adopted, I started singing "Movin' on Up," and the rest is history. FAVORITE PLACE I AM NOT SUPPOSED TO BE: Am I not supposed to be somewhere? I am not aware of any such place. FAVORITE RESTAURANT AND WHAT I ORDER: Until Americans change the law and allow us to eat in restaurants, it's Le Voltaire in Paris *pour moi*. It's red-meat heaven. MOST TROUBLE I'VE EVER GOTTEN IN: I don't get into any trouble. MY GUILTY PLEASURE: Licking Brian's and Danny's faces until they wake up. FAVORITE PLACES TO SLEEP: Far from humans who snore. SPECIAL TALENT: Is being adorable a talent? FAVORITE PLACE TO WALK: Off leash in Central Park with anyone who is awake before nine o'clock in the morning, when the leash law goes into effect. PET PEEVE: Pats on the head.

Mary McDonald's JACK, LULU, BORIS, EVA, and VIOLET

HOW WE CAME INTO OUR MOM'S LIFE: We were orphans in a shop until one day some slender arms jangling with wonderful bright things came down and swooped us up. And the rest is history. FAVORITE PLACE WE ARE NOT SUPPOSED TO BE: Anywhere outside that big white fence. FAVORITE RESTAURANT AND WHAT WE ORDER: We will go for steak frites almost anywhere. Mom says we can all go to L'Entrecôte, when it opens in L.A. MOST TROUBLE WE HAVE EVER GOTTEN IN: We used to think it was fun to make mud prints with our paws on white furniture as it looks so pretty, just like a fabric design. Mom gets mad. So it's not much fun anymore. Now there are rooms we can't go in. OUR GUILTY PLEASURES: We (Boris, Lulu, and Eva) are not sure what "guilty" means. I (Jack) like to sneak over to soft furniture to tinkle nearby. I (Violet) like to sneak out of the kitchen and hide upstairs in Mom's bed. SPECIAL TALENT: We have a howling quartet. It wins awards in the neighborhood, and even the neighbors have knocked on the door since they like it so much. FAVORITE PLACE TO WALK: Under Mom's feet. It is best when she has a lot of stuff in her hands and can't see us. PET PEEVE: Sharing attention.

Jeffrey Alan Marks's COAL

HOW I CAME INTO JEFFREY'S LIFE: I (and Chessie) came from Cherry Oaks Labradors. FAVORITE PLACE I AM NOT SUPPOSED TO BE: The walk-in pantry. FAVORITE MEAL OUT: Mastro's Steakhouse leftovers. MOST TROUBLE I'VE EVER GOTTEN IN: Once I opened up all the trash bags after my dad threw a dinner party. Oops. SPECIAL TALENT: Staying out of the rain, as I hate getting wet. FAVORITE PLACE TO WALK: Malibu Carbon Beach with my dad. PET PEEVE: Being left behind on the beach while my dad is out on his paddleboard. MY FAVORITE PLAYDATE: A beach party with my neighborhood friends.

Charlotte Moss's DAISY and BUDDY

HOW WE CAME INTO CHAR AND BARRY'S LIFE: This takes a fair amount of detective work—finding qualified humans. We had to check them out: Are we compatible? Do they read, like to entertain, travel? And how will our digs be decorated? I (Daisy) came from a breeder in Connecticut who no longer is in the business, and Ann Robbins, the current president of the Cavalier King Charles Spaniel Club, helped Char find Buddy. FAVORITE PLACE WE ARE NOT SUPPOSED TO BE: This is our house so we pretty much sit anywhere. Char and Barry are cool with that as long as we have checked our paws first. Every room seems to have these soft cashmere throws and she usually puts one on the sofa for us . . . all very cozy, and we love the colors, too. FAVORITE MEAL OUT: We have a neighborhood joint called Sette Mezzo. Char calls it our "other dining room." We pretty much stick to their spaghetti and meatballs. MOST TROUBLE BUDDY HAS EVER GOTTEN IN: When Buddy was a puppy, he was a chewer. He had the time of his life fringing the edge of a Turkish rug in the kitchen one night. Char left it that way as a reminder. Every once in a while he gets caught going for a table leg or pillow fringe. OUR GUILTY PLEA-

SURES: Buddy and I differ here. My guilty pleasure is Sunday mornings in the bed with Char. She likes to set up the bed tray with coffee (I get a treat), and then I snooze while she reads. Buddy loves it when Char gets out the brushes and combs. You should see him prance after that. Even though he is my brother, I have to admit he is a "looker." FAVORITE PLACE TO WALK: We love our dog walkers, Miss Sally and Miss Janet. We will go anywhere with them. And on the beach in the early morning with Char is pretty great.

Michelle Nussbaumer's LORETTA, TULLULAH, APOLLONIA, PASHA, WINNIE, GUMBO, LOBO, and RUPERT

HOW WE CAME INTO MICHELLE AND BERNARD'S LIFE: We were all adopted and feel really lucky. I (Pasha) like to put on airs that I am from a more pedigreed Southern background, but in reality I was rescued from the streets of New Orleans after Katrina. FAVORITE PLACE WE ARE NOT SUPPOSED TO BE: Michelle and Bernard don't have a lot of rules about that kind of thing, thank goodness. FAVORITE RESTAURANT AND WHAT WE ORDER: Starbucks because we love our Puppuccinos from their "secret" menu (whipped cream inside a small cup). FAVORITE MEAL AT HOME: Whatever Michelle is cooking as whatever she makes is so good. Chicken tagine is our favorite. MOST TROUBLE WE'VE EVER GOTTEN IN: We all agree that Apollonia is the worst, as she is always eating Italian loafers (especially Gucci). SPECIAL TALENT: We (Apollonia and Loretta) can eat right off the dining table because we are so tall. FAVORITE PLACE TO WALK AND WITH WHOM: We really like to nap—we aren't that into exercise. PET PEEVE: When Michelle makes us go outside while guests are over for dinner—so rude.

Alex Papachristidis's TEDDY

HOW I CAME INTO ALEX AND SCOTT'S LIFE: One day in July while Alex was shopping at Bergdorf Goodman, his friend CeCe Kieselstein-Cord was doing a trunk show of her posh dog apparel with her dog Tigerlily. The minute Alex saw the adorable Tigerlily, he fell in love. My dads waited two years for their perfect Yorkie puppy from CeCe's breeder, Susan Kanter. When they met my brother and me at the breeders, Scott wanted my brother, but my large ears stole Alex's heart. Alex said to Scott, "You pick the name and I will pick the dog." FAVORITE PLACE I'M NOT SUPPOSED TO BE: Rolling in something disgusting in the garden. FAVORITE MEAL AT

HOME: A little bowl full of whole milk. FAVORITE MEAL OUT: In Paris, the hamburgers at L'Avenue are scrumptious. MOST TROUBLE I'VE EVER GOTTEN IN: I am usually well behaved but sometimes I do little naughty things. MY GUILTY PLEASURE: Greenies, an edible dog treat that looks like a green toothbrush. It also cleans dogs' gums. SPECIAL TALENT: I love to sing "Happy Birthday" along with my dads and join the chorus. FAVORITE WALK AND WITH WHOM: I enjoy a beach walk with my dads and our extended family. I love to frolic with Biriba, the apricot poodle of my dad's sister, Ophelia, and her husband, Bill. PET PEEVE: Animals on television.

Katie Ridder's TEDDY

HOW I CAME INTO KATIE AND PETER'S LIFE: Katie was so upset about Tam Tam and Charlie (the dachshunds that they adopted a few months after their marriage in 1988) dying that she told Peter she was going to run errands. Instead, Katie drove to the Adirondacks and looked at puppies at the breeder. Peter called after two hours and she burst into tears, fessing up. Katie promised that she wouldn't come home with a puppy but over the course of the next week she convinced him that the family needed one, and she drove back up with the kids, Jane and Tony. The breeder told them about an older dog (me, then six months) that she thought would be better with our young kids. FAVORITE PLACE I AM NOT SUPPOSED TO BE: When I was nimbler, it was the dining room table, facing the front of the house. Now, it's among the fox droppings on the lawn. MOST TROUBLE I'VE EVER GOTTEN IN: I keep trying but my owners are fools—they forgive me for everything. FAVORITE MEAL AT HOME: Chicken liver. MY GUILTY PLEASURE: Guilt. What's that? SPECIAL TALENT: Finding opportunities with my nose. FAVORITE PLACE TO WALK: I now get pushed in a dog stroller, where I am able to smell all the wonderful scents of the neighborhood without much effort. PET PEEVE: Pedicures. I prefer not.

Carolyne Roehm's LUCKY, DUSTY, BEETHOVEN, BABY MONKEY, TROLLOP, and TEDDY BEAR

HOW WE CAME INTO CAROLYNE AND SIMON'S LIFE: It was all about our beautiful eyes. Our mom never buys or adopts a dog until she looks into his or her eyes and feels a connection. We each stared at her, and she knew it was meant to be. FAVORITE PLACE WE ARE NOT SUPPOSED TO BE: Frolicking in the mud by the lake near our property. FAVORITE MEAL: We are simple country children who like to eat at home. We are not too picky. Picking out asparagus from the vegetable patch is a favorite activity. The Weatherstone kitchen also serves us grilled steak or chicken. MOST TROUBLE WE'VE EVER GOTTEN IN: We once gave Mom a near heart attack by jumping over the fence and heading toward the street. And once, I (Trollop) ate through her cashmere shawl with lace trim. OUR GUILTY PLEASURE: Chewing on Mom's favorite shoes in the mudroom and gnawing on the stretcher of a pair of eighteenth-century English consoles. SPECIAL TALENT: I (Trollop) am athletic and intelligent. I (Monkey) am the angel who charms the world. I (Beethoven) have soulful eyes. I (Teddy) am the Esther Williams of dogs; I love doing laps in the pool. I (Dusty) weigh seven pounds but act like a Great Dane. I (Lucky) am the gatekeeper to our mom. Simon calls me her sentinel since I am never more than a few feet away from her. FAVORITE PLACE TO WALK: We love walking with Mom in the garden en route to her studio. PET PEEVE: Having to take a bath every time we roll in goose dung on our property.

Schuyler Samperton's TRICKY

HOW I CAME INTO SCHUYLER AND MARC'S LIFE: I was roaming around in the bushes of a Ralph's grocery store parking lot when I was rescued by a lovely, young couple. They knew I needed a good mom, so they introduced me to Schuyler, and it was love at first sight. FAVORITE PLACE I AM NOT SUPPOSED TO BE: I've repeatedly destroyed the upholstered Regency settee that sits in the front window. Thankfully, Brunschwig & Fils hasn't discontinued the fabric, as I just can't seem to make peace with delivery people. FAVORITE RESTAURANT AND WHAT I ORDER: A Double-Double with cheese and fries from In-N-Out is my favorite treat—especially when I'm on a road trip. FAVORITE MEAL AT HOME: I'm mad for roast chicken and have even been known to steal one or two pieces right off the table when

heads are turned. MOST TROUBLE I'VE EVER GOTTEN IN: I've never been in trouble—I don't know what that is. MY GUILTY PLEASURE: Licking empty ice-cream containers—my yummiest treat. SPECIAL TALENT: I have so many—barking on command, retrieving mail from the postman, and an uncanny understanding of the subtle nuances of human communication. FAVORITE PLACE TO WALK: I love wandering the trails of Sun Valley and running on the beach in Malibu with Schuyler. Squirrel chasing anywhere is a bonus. PET PEEVE: I loathe the vacuum cleaner, excessive heat, and when Schuyler dances.

Mark D. Sikes's LILY

HOW I CAME INTO MARK AND MICHAEL'S LIFE: I am a Southern girl, originally from Georgia. We found out about each other through friends who had adopted my sister. FAVORITE PLACE I AM NOT SUPPOSED TO BE: Sometimes when my humans are having a yoga lesson, I like to hang out right in the middle of the mats. FAVORITE RESTAURANT AND WHAT I ORDER: Tower Bar at the Sunset Tower Hotel. I order chicken or steak depending on my mood. MOST TROUBLE I'VE EVER GOTTEN IN: Sometimes I have been known to bite intruders—I mean, friends of my humans. MY GUILTY PLEASURE: House calls from my acupuncturist. I have a bad back. SPECIAL TALENT: I can snore like a truck driver. FAVORITE PLACE TO WALK: The end of our block with Michael. Any farther and I'll need to rest. PET PEEVE: Gardeners.

Windsor Smith's SUR

HOW I CAME INTO WINDSOR, ANTHONY, OLIVER, AND TRINITY'S LIFE: As a puppy, I was the resident mascot of a fraternity house. Growing tired of those beer hacks, I traded up to martini hour. FAVORITE PLACE I AM NOT SUPPOSED TO BE: In Windsor's shoe closet. FAVORITE PLACE TO SLEEP: On the cool marble in the entry foyer, which is handily also ideal for keeping watch. FAVORITE RESTAURANT AND WHAT I ORDER: I order in. Only organic, human-grade and preservative-free food from PURE Dog Food. Or a big, marrowy bone from the butcher's. MOST TROUBLE I'VE EVER GOTTEN IN: Did I mention Windsor's shoe closet? MY GUILTY PLEASURE: Cruising the Pacific Coast Highway in the front seat of a 1966 convertible Corvette. SPECIAL TALENT: I am all ears. PET PEEVE: Sirens.

Nathan Turner and Eric Hughes's NACHO and WALLY

HOW WE CAME INTO OUR DADS' LIFE: Daisy (she was our aunty) led our dads to us. She was ten years old and already living with them, and they thought she needed a companion. So they went to Cherry Oaks Labradors, where Daisy and I (Nacho) were both born. It was love at first sight for me (Nacho) but not so much with Daisy, but eventually she came around. We all miss her so much. But then came me (Wally). And now Nacho can be boss. FAVORITE PLACE WE ARE NOT SUPPOSED TO BE: Dad's Candemir daybed in his office. OUR FAVORITE OUTFIT: Dogs wear clothes? That's weird. FAVORITE PLACE TO SLEEP: We're arctic dogs living in Southern California so we like the coolest spot in the house. A cool tile floor is the best. FAVORITE RESTAURANT AND WHAT WE ORDER: I (Nacho) love going out to restaurants and staying at hotels even more. One of my favorites is the Ojai Valley Inn as they have great room service for us dogs. FAVORITE MEAL AT HOME: Chicken and peanut butter, in that order. MOST TROUBLE WE'VE EVER GOTTEN IN: It usually has to do with food. I (Nacho) once swiped an entire roast chicken fresh from the oven and ate the whole thing, bones and all, before anyone caught me. This didn't go over so well. OUR GUILTY PLEASURE: Begging for food. SPECIAL TALENT: Body surfing. FAVORITE PLACE TO WALK: We love patrolling Dog Beach with our two dads. PET PEEVE: Getting our ears cleaned . . . oh, and when Annabelle or Mai don't feed us on time. Ladies . . . five o'clock is five o'clock.

Kelly Wearstler's WILLIE

HOW I CAME INTO KELLY, BRAD, AND MY HUMAN BROTHERS' LIFE: Kelly is involved with animal rescues and hosted an adoption event at her store in 2014. I won her heart and . . . *voilà* . . . became the newest family member. FAVORITE RESTAURANT: All of the restaurants my family visits serve scrumptious food. FAVORITE MEAL AT HOME: I am treated to chicken strips once a week and on special occasions. Deelish. MY FAVORITE OUTFIT: I prefer going *au naturel*. L.A. is so sunny and predictable. When it's hot in the city, I like to swim at the beach. Clothes are a hassle unless I need to impress. Then my V-neck pink cable-knit sweater works magic. MOST TROUBLE I'VE EVER GOTTEN IN: It is a shame that Mom's shoes taste so good. MY GUILTY PLEASURE: Sometimes other humans in Malibu leave their doors to the beach wide open. Doesn't that mean that I am welcome to come in and say hello? SPECIAL TALENT: I can snarl a lot when I play and get really loud. FAVORITE PLACE TO WALK: My brothers, Oliver and Elliott, like to let me loose and play along the beach. They can't catch me no matter how loudly they yell, "Willie!" PET PEEVE: Getting bathed regularly is for the birds. What is so wrong with the way I smell?

Hutton Wilkinson's PIPER and KIPPY

HOW WE CAME INTO OUR MOM AND DAD'S LIFE: We were selected from West Highland white terrier breeder Shirley Jean Neihaus's Whitehaus Kennels. As brother and sister from the same parents, we were born from different litters a year apart. FAVORITE PLACE WE ARE NOT SUPPOSED TO BE: We never let our parents go under the bed or up on the sofa pillows, as this is reserved especially for us. I (Piper) like to help my dad redecorate by knocking the pillow off every chair and sofa onto the floor. I can't figure out why he doesn't realize they look better that way. MOST TROUBLE WE HAVE EVER GOTTEN IN: I (Kippy) remember the time that Piper peed on the bedroom carpet and my mom thought I did it but I didn't do it. I (Piper) didn't pee on the bedroom carpet. Kippy is a liar. I only pooped on the carpet. OUR GUILTY PLEASURES: I (Kippy) like helping my mom in the garden by digging up the tulip bulbs right after she plants them. I (Piper) like to pull the toilet paper off the roll and then watch Kippy take the blame. SPECIAL TALENT: My (Piper) special trick is to never return a ball or a toy if it's thrown for me, and I only come if someone grabs my collar and leads me. I (Kippy) like to eat. I can clean a plate in record time and then eat whatever's left in Piper's dish too. I can also sing, but I don't think my parents really appreciate my contralto.

Bunny Williams's ANABELLE and BEBE

HOW WE CAME INTO BUNNY AND JOHN'S LIFE: They found us on PetFinder.com. FAVORITE PLACE WE ARE NOT SUPPOSED TO BE: We are not supposed to run through the garden beds but they are so hard to resist . . . especially when we see a chipmunk running through the plants to escape us. MOST TROUBLE WE'VE EVER GOTTEN IN: Our obligation to protect Bunny and John can be a little terrifying but our new bark collars seem to be telling us to stop the noise. SPECIAL TALENT: The best thing we do is love Bunny and John.

SOME FAVORITE RESOURCES AND ANIMAL CHARITIES

Resources

ON CLEANING UP

Get Serious!
www.getseriousproducts.net
Stain, odor, and pheromone extractor that's quick and easy to use.

Nature's Miracle
www.naturesmiracle.com
Accidents, grass stains, mud, vomit, and odors are no match for this bio-enzymatic cleaning formula.

poopbags
www.poopbags.com
Made with plants and compostable.

ON DINING

Darwins
www.darwinspet.com
Raw pet food delivered to your door.

Fetch
www.fetchdog.com
Offers everything from fancy feed stations to personalized dinner mats for your dog.

Greenies
www.greenies.com
Great mint dental daily chew treats for dogs' teeth.

Petco
www.petco.com
Has every brand of food and treat for every size and breed of dog.

Pure Vita
www.purevitapetfoods.com
Pet formula made with natural, holistic ingredients (with added vitamins and minerals).

Pure Dog Food
www.puredogfood.com
Human-grade natural and organic dog food with an easy-to-use delivery service in the Los Angeles area.

ON FINDING A FRIEND

Adopt-a-Pet.com
www.adoptapet.com
Search online for dogs who need homes: choose any size, age, or breed.

Petfinder
www.petfinder.com
Pets available for adoption.

ON GETTING GROOMED

Earthbath All-Natural Pet Shampoo
www.earthbath.com
Totally natural, 100% biodegradable and cruelty-free shampoo in a wide range of fragrances.

Hertzko Self-Cleaning Slicker Brush
www.hertzko.com
Gently removes loose hair and eliminates tangles, knots, dander, and trapped dirt.

ON LOUNGING

Ballard Designs
www.ballarddesigns.com
Offers durable and stylish outdoor/indoor rugs and fabric by the yard.

Orvis
www.orvis.com
Grip-tight furniture protectors and reversible dog-proof matching coverlets and shams for dog beds.

Pottery Barn
www.potterybarn.com
Their faux-fur throws are cozy for pets, chic to look at, and protect furniture.

Rough n' Rowdy by Perennials
www.perennialsfabrics.com
Acrylic fabric that looks like thick-weight linen yet stands up to dogs' paws.

ON SLEEPING

Fatboy
www.fatboyusa.com
Their fun range of doggie lounges are produced in a strong nylon material that repels moisture and shuts out unpleasant odors.

Frontgate
www.frontgate.com
Create a custom dog bed, including orthopedic and senior dog options.

WallyBed
www.wallybed.com
Dozens of styles and options, including one that is self-contained with no zipper or cover to remove before machine washing and drying.

ON TRAVELING

Harry Barker
www.harrybarker.com
From leopard travel food storage bags and dog toile blankets to portable water bowls, they have it all.

L.L. Bean
www.llbean.com
Their boat and tote is the ideal way to carry your dog's life to and fro and can be monogrammed.

Puppia
www.puppiaus.com
Their best-selling soft mesh harness is ideal for small dogs.

Rescue Relief
www.bachrescueremedypet.com
Natural stress relief for pets when they travel.

Urban Pup
www.urbanpup.com
Chic travel options, from a faux black croc carrier to a dog seat and dog cradle.

ON WEARING

The Artful Canine
www.theartfulcanine.com
Custom dog collars, leashes, and dog ID tags.

Bella Bean
www.bellabeancouture.com
A whimsical line of dog accessories.

Dog Collars Boutique
www.dogcollarsboutique.com
Hand-beaded leather dog collars and leads made in Kenya.

Found My Animal
www.foundmyanimal.com
Leashes and collars with a unique nautical twist.

Ralph Lauren
www.ralphlauren.com
A wide range of signature clothing, from polo shirts to tartan wool-blend dog coats.

Wagwear
www.wagwear.com
Very fashion-forward canine clothing, from doggie denim mini backpacks to dip-dyed collars.

Ware of the Dog
www.wareofthedog.com
A luxury dog accessory collection that works with artists and craftsmen to create special one-of-a-kind items.

Animal Charities

American Society for the Prevention of Cruelty to Animals® (ASPCA)
www.aspca.org

Animal Medial Center of New York City (AMC)
www.amcny.org

Animal Rescue Fund of the Hamptons (ARF)
www.arfhamptons.org

Autism Service Dogs of America (ASDA)
www.autismservicedogsofamerica.com

Best Friends Animal Society
www.bestfriends.org

Danny and Ron's Rescue
www.dannyandronsrescue.com

Guide Dogs for the Blind
www.guidedogs.com

Have a Heart Animal Welfare Fund
www.haveaheartanimalwelfare.org

Hooves and Paws Animal Rescue
www.hoovesandpaws.org

Hope For Paws
www.hopeforpaws.org

Independent Labrador Retriever Rescue of Southern California (Indi Lab Rescue)
www.indilabrescue.org

The Little Guild of St. Francis
www.littleguild.org

No-Kill Los Angeles (NKLA)
www.nkla.org

North Shore Animal League of America
www.animalleague.org

Paws with a Cause
www.pawswithacause.org

The Rescue Train
www.therescuetrain.org

Thrive Animal Rescue
www.thriveanimalrescue.com

Wags and Walks
www.wagsandwalks.org

Robert Couturier's Hercule sits on a Louis XVI musician chair upholstered in Prelle silk velvet in front of a Jean-Michel Frank straw marquetry screen.

ACKNOWLEDGMENTS

At Home with Dogs and Their Designers would not be half as stylish nor as delightful without Stacey Bewkes's insightful, artful eye as its main photographer. Stacey embraced this major challenge of never having shot a book before with her signature dedication, intelligence, and passion for all things design (not to mention dogs) like she had been doing it all her life. To say I am beyond grateful is a massive understatement. To say we had fun doing this together feels equally inadequate.

Cher Robert Couturier: Your love for your dogs is the heartbeat behind this book and the inspiration for it. *Mille mercis* for your wonderful foreword.

Sandy Gilbert and Charles Miers: You trusted me with this idea and I feel so lucky to be able to bring it to life. Once again, thank you for giving me the honor of being published by Rizzoli.

Jason Snyder: You rocked the layout with your signature pizazz and patience. Thank you.

Steven Gambrel: You uttered the unique phrase that became the title of this book when we were shooting you and Sailor, and I have gratefully held onto it ever since.

Bernard Lucien Nussbaumer: You captured your one-and-only wife and your furry brood on camera when we couldn't be there. Her chapter makes the book that much more stylish. Thank you so much for your time and talent.

And finally: Infinite gratitude goes to all the wonderful dogs and their designers who are featured herein. You opened your homes to us so enthusiastically and graciously. We are so excited to share your special bond with each other to the world.

OPPOSITE

Katie Ridder and Teddy stroll into their Greek Revival–inspired retreat in Millbrook, New York. This residential building was designed by Peter Pennoyer Architects.

First published in the United States of America in 2017
by Rizzoli International Publications, Inc.
300 Park Avenue South
New York, New York 10010
www.rizzoliusa.com

Text © 2017 Susanna Salk

All photography © 2017 by Stacey Bewkes, with the exception of images taken by Melanie Acevedo © 2017 page 140, Brittany Ambridge © 2017 page 76, Bernard Lucien Nussbaumer © 2017 pages 84–89, Simon Pinniger © 2017 page 110 (bottom right), Jean Randazzo © 2017 pages 62–69 and 166 (middle left), and Susanna Salk © 2017 page 8. *It's a Dog's Life* iPhone images were provided by the designers unless otherwise noted. The following images in this section were taken by Stacey Bewkes © 2017: pages 163 (bottom left), 165 (bottom right), 167 (top left), 168 (right), 170 (top left), and 171 (middle and bottom left).

2017 2018 2019 2020 /10 9 8 7 6 5 4 3 2 1

Printed in China

ISBN 13: 978-0-8478-6090-6

Library of Congress Control Number: 2017942294

Project Editor: Sandra Gilbert
Editorial Assistant provided by Hilary Ney and Elizabeth Smith
Production Manager: Alyn Evans
Book Design: Jason Snyder

Credits:
Thank you to the textile companies and the designers for allowing us to reproduce their fabrics throughout this book. Jonathan Adler: Crawford in Camel by Jonathan Adler; Martyn Lawrence Bullard: Kubla Mini in Fog by Martyn Lawrence Bullard; Betsy Burnham: Buckley Plaid by Jane Shelton; Robert Couturier: Christopher Hyland's Flame Stitch in Multicolored; Steven Gambrel: Maori in tang brown, tan, black, and pale beige from Fortuny, Inc.; Brooke Giannetti: Chinese Scenic by Gracie; Brian McCarthy: Clarence House's Hoffman Velvet in Red; Mary McDonald: Bermuda Blossoms in Jet by Mary McDonald for Schumacher; Jeffrey Alan Marks: Spiro in River by Jeffrey Alan Marks for Kravet; Charlotte Moss: Digby's Tent in Moss by Charlotte Moss for Brunschwig & Fils; Michelle Nussbaumer: Chevron Ikat by Michelle Nussbaumer; Alex Papachristidis: Le Manach Silk Velvet Leopard by Pierre Frey; Katie Ridder: Turtle Bay in Seafoam by Katie Ridder Inc.; Carolyne Roehm: Sohil Crewel in Indigo by Lee Jofa; Schuyler Samperton: Odhna by Shyam Ahuja; Mark Sikes: Bel Air Stripe in Cobalt by Mark D. Sikes for Schumacher; Windsor Smith: Kaveka designed by Windsor Smith for Kravet; Nathan Turner: Malibu from Nathan Turner wallpaper with Wallshoppe; Kelly Wearstler: Avant fabric in Linen Off White by Kelly Wearstler; Hutton Wilkinson: Jim Thompson Gemstone in Emerald, Tony Duquette Collection designed by Hutton Wilkinson; Bunny Williams: Bunny Williams for Lee Jofa "Isabella" in Gold/Olive.

Pages 2–3: Interior designer Betsy Burnham in her Los Angeles garden with her devotees.

Page 4: Designer Carolyne Roehm in her Connecticut garden with some of her beloved dogs.